The Daily Telegraph

The Cotswolds

in a week

GABRIELLE MACPHEDRAN

D0293374

Headway • Hodder & Stoughton

Acknowledgements

The author and publishers are grateful to the following for permission to reproduce photographs in this volume:

J Allan Cash Ltd: Front cover; Stroud District Council: Back cover; Bath Tourism Marketing: p 117; Berkeley Castle: p 94; Elaine Rippon p 42; Forestry Commission: p 105; Gloucester City Council pp 44, 61, 64, 84, 100, 102, 103; Prinknash Abbey p 70; Wildfowl & Wetlands Trust, Slimbridge: p 98.

All other photographs taken by the author

Maps created by Alan Gilliland and Glenn Swann

Front cover: River Coln at Quenington
Back cover: St Mary's Mill, Chalford

British Library Cataloguing in Publication Data
Macphedran, Gabrielle
"Daily Telegraph" The Cotswolds in a Week
("Daily Telegraph" Travel in a Week Series)
I. Title II. Series
914.241704

ISBN 0 340 58314 2

First published 1993

Impression number	10	9	8	7	6	5	4	3	2	
Year		1998	1997	1996	1995	1994	1993			

Printed in Italy for the educational publishing division of Hodder & Stoughton Ltd, Mill Road, Dunton Green, Sevenoaks, Kent TN13 2YA by New Interlitho, Milan.

THE COTSWOLDS IN A WEEK

Introduction

This guide is designed for visitors touring the Cotswolds by car who wish to see the best the region has to offer in the limited time at their disposal. We have divided the Cotswolds into seven areas, each of which can easily be covered in a day's drive. Within each of these 'Days' the most interesting sights, from country homes and nature parks to the best of Bath, Cheltenham and Gloucester, have been listed as a menu of options, arranged in alphabetical order for easy reference. From the Day's menu you can choose the attractions which hold most appeal, depending on the weather, your interests, and whether you are travelling with children. Symbols placed alongside the text will aid you in your choice.

There are hundreds of attractions open to the public in the Cotswolds and the aim of this guide is to give a critical appraisal of the most popular and help you discover some of the region's hidden gems. Our assessments of the different sights and attractions will give you a clear idea of what you can expect to see, the best time of day and year to pay a visit and, where admission is charged, whether the attractions offer value for money. As well as covering the main towns and tourist honeypots, we have highlighted small gems in each area, from artisans' workshops and craft centres to historic churches and good places for lunch.

A walk of the day in each area is described in detail. Most are just over one hour long and provide an opportunity to get out of the car and stretch your legs. We have also included descriptions of particularly interesting drives which are scenic in both rain and sunshine. At the end of each Day we have given suggestions for places to stay, from country house hotels to farmhouses, and places to eat, from the best restaurants to pubs serving good home-made fare.

CONTENTS

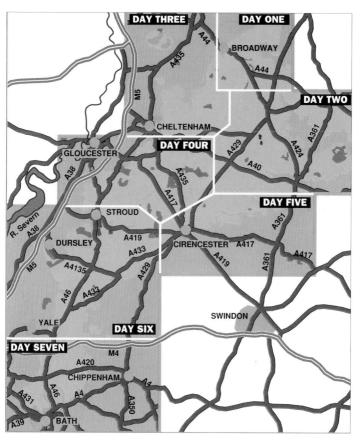

KEY TO SYMBOLS

- ✪ Star Attraction
- ☆ Well worth a visit
- ☆ Of interest
- ‼ Walk of the day
- ---- Route of walk
- 🚗 Drive of the day
- ═══ Route of drive
- ☀ Fine weather attraction
- 🌧 Wet weather attraction
- 🏃 Enjoyable for children
- ⓘ Tourist Information Centre
- ◉ Lunch/snack stop
- 🏨 Hotel
- Ĝ Guesthouse
- ꜱᴄ Self-catering accommodation
- ✕ Restaurant
- 🍺 Pub with good food
- 🍺 Pub with accommodation

- 👦5 Children allowed (number = from which age)
- 🐕 Dogs allowed
- 💳 Credit cards accepted
- 💳̸ Credit cards not accepted
- £ Bed and breakfast under £17 per person; three-course meal under £10 a head
- ££ Bed and breakfast £18-£35 per person; three-course meal £11-£16 a head
- £££ Bed and breakfast £36-£49 per person; three-course meal £17-£24 a head
- ££££ Bed and breakfast over £50 per person; three-course meal over £25 a head

1

THE GOLDEN
TOWNS

Chipping Campden, Moreton-in-Marsh and Broadway - towns that are almost a shorthand for the Cotswolds - lie close to one another in the north-east. Each is subtly different. Moreton-in-Marsh is a properly lived-in, honest-to-goodness little town, Broadway is breathtakingly pretty, despite the traffic jams, while Chipping Campden is stately and golden.

The situation of the towns is very different - Broadway lies almost outside the Cotswold Hills at the foot of the escarpment which marks their beginning in the west; Chipping Campden is hidden in a valley at the northern end of the plateau, while Moreton follows the gentle tilt of land out of the wolds to the east.

The towns themselves are not the only attraction. Garden lovers can combine a visit to the National Trust Hidcote Manor Garden, with Kiftsgate garden just five minutes' walk away, or explore Batsford Arboretum just outside Moreton-in-Marsh. If the weather looks uncertain, this part of the Cotswolds also has a number of fine country houses, several of them monuments to English eccentricity. Snowshill Manor is not only pretty in the way of Cotswold manor houses, its museum is a most idiosyncratic and hugely entertaining jumble, the lifetime collection of super-magpie Charles Wade.

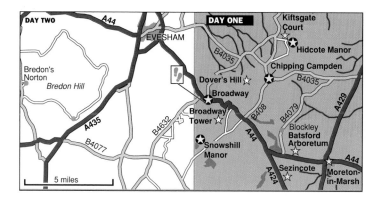

The northern escarpment of the Cotswolds rises high in these parts and on a fine day there are incomparable views - choose from Broadway Tower Country Park or Dover's Hill, both excellent spaces for children to let off steam. From these lofty, windblown heights, the land tumbles and rolls in soft wooded hills; fields are criss-crossed by low hedges and dry stone walls; grey stone houses cluster beside the stream in the shadow of the parish church and the manor house.

Distances are not great in the Cotswolds and the scale is almost domestic. Having made a base, the best way to explore is on foot. The Cotswold Way, the long distance footpath running along the escarpment from Bath to Chipping Campden, would take the steady walker at least a week to complete. But it is quite possible to dip into some of its most attractive stretches, many of which lie in this northern region.

☆ BATSFORD ARBORETUM

There are over 1,500 different species of trees and shrubs planted in these 50 acres of gently sloping hillside above the Evenlode valley. A falconry centre and an owl wood provide the fauna to accompany the flora.

Most people come for the trees, many of them exotic and rare. There are varieties of the more familiar species of cedar, redwood, bamboo, oak, sorbus, acer and over 60 types of magnolia. Most of the trees and bushes are labelled and you need to buy the guide (£1) to explain what you are seeing.

The garden was created in the 1880s by Bertie Mitford, 1st Lord Redesdale (grandfather of the Mitford sisters) after he retired from a career as a diplomat. Much of his career was spent in Japan and China, hence the Japanese resthouse and bronze buddha and Oriental temple. It is now owned and run by Lord Dulverton who lives nearby at Batsford House (not open to the public).

The Apple Store tea-room serves cakes (mostly home-made), sandwiches and light lunches, tea and coffee. You can sit inside or out on the terrace overlooking the garden centre which sells a good variety of plants and trees. Both the tea-room and garden centre shop can get crowded on summer weekends. The picnic area is quieter.

The **Cotswold Falconry Centre**, situated in this park, has displays of eagles, hawks, falcons and owls in flight, accompanied by a running commentary. Younger children can become seriously bored but older siblings enjoy the chance to handle the birds. The Centre runs a serious breeding and conservation programme for rare birds of prey, and an Owl Wood, where the chief attraction is the breeding of barn owls for release into the wild.

Batsford Arboretum, Batsford, Moreton-in-Marsh - access from A44 only.
Tel: 0386 700409
Opening times: Arboretum - daily Good Fri-end Oct/early Nov, depending on when the autumn colours have reached their peak, 10am-5pm. Falconry Centre - daily Mar-Nov 10.30am-5pm
Admission: adult £2; child 10-16 £1.50
Garden Centre - tel: 0386 700409. Open daily all year 10am-5pm

✪ BROADWAY

The mellow golden stone of the northern Cotswold towns is seen at its best here in Broadway, particularly on summer evenings. The houses with steep, lichen-covered gables follow the sweep and curve of the broad main street to the village green. Cottage gardens are rampant with roses and hollyhocks behind dry stone walls. Be warned: Broadway is on everyone's itinerary.

In the 16th century, Broadway was a thriving coach terminus on the London-Worcester run. Horses had to be changed before

A summer scene in Broadway

they could tackle steep Fish Hill to the south of town and shops and inns grew up to meet the needs of weary travellers. During the railway age of the 19th century, the town fell into a decline until William Morris (1834-1896) and his comrades of the Arts and Crafts Movement came looking for the lost innocence of a vanishing rural England. Craftsmen settled here, rebuilding Broadway in the best traditions of English workmanship and design. The town we see today is largely their legacy.

The Lygon Arms Hotel is at the centre of the town. A 16th-century manor house turned coaching inn, it enjoyed an Arts and Crafts facelift in the 1920s and is now one of the premier Cotswold hotels (see also Where to Stay). The North Cotswold Hunt sets off from here throughout the hunting season which begins on the last Saturday in September.

> **Hampers Delicatessen** in the shopping precinct, Cotswold Court, will pack you a picnic ploughman's lunch for £4. If you prefer smoked salmon and Champagne (half a bottle), it'll be £25 for two. Open every day from mid-March to Christmas.

One of Broadway's oldest and finest buildings is **Abbot's Grange**, a former monastic house of the 14th century, standing at the end of the green on Church Street.

After its good looks, Broadway's speciality is shops. Many are open every day of the week selling expensive antique furniture, pictures, prints, Scottish woollen sweaters and any number of useless but no doubt amusing gifts. Locals hanker after a super-market. The **Tourist Information Centre** (0386 852937) is open from Easter to the end of October.

BROADWAY WALK

This walk, for which you should allow an hour, takes you away from the crowds through the fields behind the town to the love-ly Norman **Church of St Eadburgha**. Take the narrow alley beside H W Keil's antique showrooms, signposted to the Old Church. Cross three fields of rough pasture along the bottom of a wide valley. This brings you out on the metalled road near the entrance to Lybrook Farm. Continue a few yards further along the road to the Old Church.

There is no electric light or heating so the church is open to visi-tors only from April to October and for Evensong at 6.30pm on Sundays from June to September. Look out for the almsbox, about 800 years old, with three locks, one for the vicar, one for each of the church wardens, and an unusual late 19th-century coffin cart with solid wheels. The churchyard, full of holly, yew and chestnut, is bordered by a field and stream with hills rising up the other side. Directly opposite St Eadburgha's, a wide leafy footpath leads to the top of Broadway Tower.

Return to the town by the metalled road passing the new church, that is to say the Victorian church of St Michael, on your right, and then The Crown and Trumpet, the pub most used by locals.

BROADWAY TOWER COUNTRY PARK

A steep climb on foot or five minutes by car from the centre of Broadway brings you to Broadway Beacon, one of the highest points in the Cotswolds. Here, at the very top of Broadway Country Park, stands Broadway Tower, a stone folly built in 1798 by James Wyatt for the 6th Earl of Coventry. The views

Broadway Tower

Chipping Campden High Street

from this windswept hilltop are tremendous, and, from the top of the Tower, some say you can see 12 counties.

There is a small permanent exhibition on each of the three upper floors of the tower, none of them riveting. One tells the history of the tower itself, another is dedicated to William Morris who occasionally stayed here with his friends of the pre-Raphaelite movement, Burne-Jones and Rossetti, and the last has a few displays about Cotswold sheep.

The Country Park also has a children's farmyard with goats, bantams and rabbits, and an adventure playground with trampoline and climbing frames and some nature trails which will amuse younger children. The Rookery Barn Restaurant serves mediocre snacks.

Broadway Tower Country Park, Fish Hill, Broadway - off the A44. Tel: 0386 852390
Opening times: daily Apr 1-Oct 31 10am-6pm
Admission: adult £2.50; child £1.50

If you are looking for a water nymph, roaring lions or the definitive garden gnome, look no further. **Architectural Heritage** sells garden statuary (antique and reproduction) and stained glass. Find them at Taddington Manor, Taddington, nr Cutsdean, on a minor road between Broadway and Snowshill (tel: 038673 414).

Statuary for sale at Architectural Heritage

⭐ CHIPPING CAMPDEN

This most serious and substantial of Cotswold towns is also one of the loveliest, particularly seen from the crest of the hills that enfold it. Its long and winding High Street has an unbroken line of grey-gold houses dating from the 14th to 17th centuries.

The houses are mostly inns, restaurants and shops now but their steeply pitched gables, tall chimneys and mullioned windows remain to delight all visitors. Unlike Broadway, there are few car parks, and coach tours avoid the town.

'Chipping', the Old English word for 'market', refers to the market in wool, the prized commodity that brought traders here from the Low Countries and Italy. The oldest house in town, **Grevel House**, was built at the end of the 14th century for a rich

Market at Chipping Campden

wool merchant of that name. Notice the unusual two-storey window and the high arched doorway to accommodate packhorses loaded with fleeces. The **Woolstaplers Hall**, another 14th-century building, now houses a **Tourist Information Centre** (tel: 0386 840101), closed in the winter, and a strange higgledy-piggledy museum of domestic artefacts ranging from man traps to artificial legs and typewriters.

The spacious **Parish Church of St James** was built with the proceeds of the woollen trade. You will see William Grevel's memorial brass on the floor of the chancel, which describes him as 'the flower of all the wool merchants of England'. Here, too, is the monstrously grand marble tomb of Sir Baptist Hicks, later Lord Campden, a man of such substance that he could lend money to King James I and half his court. He was also a great benefactor. The almshouses near the church and the covered Market Hall in the middle of the High Street are among his bequests to the people of Campden which are still standing - unlike his own mansion, burnt down by Royalist forces in the Civil War, leaving only two small lodges and a gatehouse.

A quiet place to sit or have a picnic is the small but attractive **Ernest Wilson Memorial Garden**, in the High Street towards the north end of town, overlooked by the church tower. Wilson, born in Campden in 1876, set up the arboretum at Harvard University.

Chipping Campden, like Broadway, benefited from the rural diaspora of the Arts and Crafts Movement. The silversmith George Hart arrived here in 1902 from the East End of London. His grandson, David, can be visited at the same premises, an old silk mill in Sheep Street where he still makes silverware by hand. Confusingly, the major sign outside reads *Pyments*, and in smaller letters underneath *David Hart, Silversmith*. His work is displayed in churches and museums but he will also accept private commissions. Open from 9am-5pm (Saturday 9am-noon).

Robert Welch, the notable industrial designer and silversmith, has premises on an upper floor of the same building. His work is often displayed in museums worldwide, including the V&A in London, and he sells his own designs of kitchenware, cutlery, glass and silver from his shop, Robert Welch Studio Shop, on the corner of Lower High Street and Sheep Street. Open Monday-Saturday, 9am-5pm.

☆ DOVER'S HILL

This is a lofty place on the edge of the north Cotswolds, good for spreading out a rug and enjoying a picnic. From this perch you can look down over hills dotted with fat sheep, across the Vale of Evesham to the Malvern Hills and Wales beyond. This was once the venue for the 17th-century Cotswold Olympick Games and the hill is named after their founder, Robert Dover.

The games, held during the Whitsun Week, consisted of horse racing, wrestling, jumping, shin kicking (training for this involved beating one's own shins with a stick to harden them). These events grew more and more boisterous and the games were abolished in the mid-19th century.

If you are here over the weekend of the Spring Bank Holiday, be sure to attend the modern version. There's wrestling, hill running, tossing sheaves of corn over various obstacles, tugs-of-war, a huge bonfire and fireworks, followed by a torchlight procession winding down the hill to Chipping Campden. The festivities end with a stirring address by a modern Robert Dover, and dancing in the square.

✪ HIDCOTE MANOR GARDEN

This most famous of Cotswold gardens was nothing more than a few rough fields at the turn of the century. It took 40 years for the American horticulturalist Major Lawrence Johnston, using many of the ideas of earlier English gardeners like Gertrude Jekyll and William Robinson, to transform it into one of the loveliest in England. Vita Sackville-West, who later created her own garden at Sissinghurst Castle in Kent, was a frequent visitor and wrote the introduction to the official guide to Hidcote.

Hidcote is designed as a series of inter-connecting plots, each with its own distinctive colour, function, or genus of flower - the Japanese garden, the water garden, the white garden and so on. But expect profusion and richness rather than regimentation (Gertrude Jekyll could not abide the sight of bare earth in any flower bed in summer). It is a garden of surprises, where you turn and catch the sudden unexpected view or find yourself in a secret wooded corner. The straight lines of fruit trees and hedges (yew, oak with hornbeam, copper beach) and grey stone walls are a perfect foil for the colour and extravagance of the flower borders, best seen in early summer.

Hidcote attracts a formidable army of gardening experts as well as those who just want to see 'a nice show'. The crowds on summer weekends become uncomfortably dense and there may be some waiting, even pushing and shoving, as you pass from one part of the garden to another. Avoid Bank Holidays but don't expect solitude here, at any time. There is an official guide book and a cheaper fold-out plan on sale. The plan simply divides the garden into sections, listing the plants in each. But as the plants are rarely labelled, its use is limited.

The garden centre stocks the range of plants you would find in any good garden shop. Gentians are very popular and the more unusual *tropaeolium speciosum*, Scottish flame flower, sells very well. The restaurant serves good simple lunches and home-made cakes for tea.

Hidcote Manor Garden, Hidcote Bartrim - access from B4081. Tel: 0386 438333
Opening times: Easter Sat-end Oct, daily except Tues & Fri, 11am-6pm or 1 hr before sunset
Admission: adult £3.90; child £1.90

Hidcote Manor Garden

☆ KIFTSGATE COURT GARDEN

Five minutes' walk down the hill from Hidcote brings you to another superb garden, Kiftsgate Court, created shortly after the First World War, at about the same time as Hidcote. There was probably a regular traffic of ideas and cuttings between the two.

Kiftsgate is built on a more intimate, domestic scale than its grander neighbour. It grows densely round a fine house which looks entirely neo-classical but is actually Victorian, with an 18th-century façade borrowed from another manor house. House and garden stand on the edge of a dramatically steep escarpment overlooking the Vale of Evesham. Rare cistus, viburnum and roses - including the famous Kiftsgate Rose, over 60 ft tall and covered in masses of white flowers - are the specialities here.

There is an explanatory leaflet for 40p but if you want the map as well, you'll have to splash out £1 on the guide book. Most plants are clearly labelled. The best time to visit is early summer.

The garden centre is rather informal. A few trestle tables outside the house have plants for sale including the Kiftsgate rose, some rare phlox, hostas and hibiscus. Inside the house, the small tea room is open only in the summer. The rest of the building is closed to the public.

Kiftsgate Court Garden, nr Chipping Campden - access from B4081. Tel: 0386 438777
Opening times: Apr 1-end Sept, Sun, Wednes, Thurs and Bank Hol Mons 2-6pm
Admission: adult £2.20; child 80p

☆ MORETON-IN-MARSH

The best thing about Moreton-in-Marsh is a feature common to all Cotswold towns: the lovely buttercream-coloured stone houses on either side of a wide - in this case, tree-lined - road. This is a proper town, with a life of its own, a busy Tuesday market and a number of good restaurants. Some residents commute to London (Lord Redesdale knew what he was doing back in the dawn of the railway age when he insisted all trains should stop in Moreton). Rare in this neck of the northern Cotswolds, the banks have cash dispensers.

Grey-gold stone houses

Rather like Broadway, it grew up as a coaching stop at an inter-
section of major roads. There's nothing much to see here, it's just
a pleasant place to be. The oldest monument is the 16th-century
Curfew Tower on the corner of Oxford Street, used as the town
lock-up until the last century.

St James Restaurant and Pâtisserie in the High Street, a recent
arrival in Moreton, is open for coffee and cakes and meals every
day from 10am until 10pm (8pm on Sundays). The speciality of
the house is good cheer and a presumption that people feel hun-
gry at any time of day. The food is excellent and reasonably
priced. A ploughman's lunch comes with game pie, local cheese,
home-made chutney and pickled onions, for £3.75. There is a
choice of vegetarian dishes. Evening meals are also served. The
house wine is Australian and the choice of beers ranges from
Spanish San Miguel to Canadian Labatt.

☆ SEZINCOTE

This is a splendid house in landscaped gardens - on the face of it,
hardly a rarity in the Cotswolds. But Sezincote is unusual in
being an Oriental-looking mansion - complete with onion domes,
spiky finials and verandah - set in a typical Cotswold landscape.
The poet John Betjeman knew Sezincote well as a young man. He
called it the 'Nabob's House', a reference to the original owner of
the house, Charles Cockerell, who made his fortune working for
the East India Company at the end of the 18th century. Cockerell
commissioned his brother, Samuel Pepys Cockerell, another old
India hand, to build Sezincote for him when he came home to
England, and it became a model for the Brighton Pavilion.

The house and grounds fell into neglect until the estate was
bought by the Kleinwort banking family in the 1940s and
restored to its former glory. The grounds are delightful, with
green sweeps of hill descending to lake and river. It's worth pay-
ing for entry into the grounds even if you don't step inside the
house.

By contrast with its sub-Moghul exterior, the interior of the
house is in deeply classical (that is, English 18th-century) style -

with a broad staircase leading to the state rooms on the first floor, splendid with high coved ceiling, gilt mirrors and huge bay windows. The decoration is by Colefax and Fowler, supervised by John Fowler himself, with clever use of paint effects and *trompe-l'oeil*. A lovely mural of Indian scenes is painted around the circular walls of the dining room. Guided tours of the house, on the hour and half hour, are useful and informative.

Sezincote Gardens, Sezincote, nr Moreton-in-Marsh – signposted from A44.
Tel: 0386 700444
Opening times: all year except Dec - Thurs, Fri and Bank Hol Mon 2-6pm (or dusk if earlier)
Admission: adult £2; child £1 (no dogs)
The House is open May, June, Jul & Sept - Thurs and Fri 2.30-5.30pm
Admission: £3; no children

❂ SNOWSHILL MANOR

A tour of this 16th-century Cotswold manor house generally has the visitor bursting with curiosity to know more about its last owner, Charles Paget Wade. The house's extraordinary contents - bizarre, beautiful, mysterious, amusing - remain much as he left them, all displayed as he intended when he gave the house to the National Trust. The only addition is electric light.

Wade was a craftsman and architect. He saw an advertisement for Snowshill Manor in an old copy of *Country Life* magazine in France at the end of the First World War. On his return, he bought and restored it, then began to fill it with 'many things of everyday use in the past, of small value, but of interest as records of various handicrafts'. These include dolls, clocks, prams, bicycles, carved chests, Chinese lacquered tables, masks, musical instruments, costumes, globes, drums and craftsmen's tools.

The objects, which are of all ages, came from all over the world and, apart from the larger collections like tools or armour, are arranged in no particular chronological or thematic order. Wade's only condition was that every object on display should reach his own standard of perfection in design, colour and workmanship - shades of the Arts and Crafts tradition.

The Green Room is most dramatic, full of models of Japanese Samurai warriors in 17th- to 19th-century armour, displayed as though preparing for battle: swords drawn and banners raised.

Even with contemporary lighting, they still create an effect worthy of Wade himself. He was clearly a tremendously theatrical character, often slipping away from his guests in the middle of a candlelit tour, to reappear minutes later from another direction, dressed in 17th-century costume, to resume the conversation. As his collection grew bigger, he had to move into an adjoining building, the Priest's House. His workshop is still here along with his spartan cupboard bed. He died in 1956; some of the attendants at Snowshill Manor still remember him.

The small terraced garden was designed by Wade's friend Baillie Scott and for the last few years, the National Trust has been experimenting with it as their first non-chemical garden. Progress is steady, they say. Note Wade's choice of blue/grey in the garden and the fine dovecote with nest boxes for 380 birds.

Traditionally, dovecotes, or, in plain language, pigeon houses could be built only on land belonging to the lord of the manor. Birds were an important source of protein for the whole commu-

St George the Bellringer at Snowshill Manor

Dovecote and millstone

nity in winter but the peasants were not only denied pigeon pie, they had to suffer their lordship's pigeons feeding on their crops.

Snowshill Manor, Snowshill - access from A44 in Broadway. Tel: 0386 852410
Opening times: Apr-end Oct - Sat, Sun and Easter Mon 11am-1pm & 2-5pm; May-end Sept - Wednes-Sun and Bank Hol Mons 11am-1pm & 2-6pm. Entry may be restricted on very busy days
Admission: adult £3.80; child £1.90; family ticket (2 adults, 4 children) £10.40

WHERE TO STAY

Blockley
🏠 ✕ 🧍 🐕 ▭ **£££**

The Crown Inn and Hotel, *High Street, Blockley, Moreton-in-Marsh, Glos GL56 9EX*
Tel: 0386 700245
Open all year
This 16th-century coaching inn has always been a popular eating place. Now, it has newly restored accommodation of 21 bedrooms, including two four-poster suites. All bedrooms have bathrooms and the usual colour TV, radio, hairdryer an hospitality tray. The decoration and furnishing is pleasant and cofortable rather than the last word in elegance and luxury. The service is friendly and the atmosphere in the lounges and bars convivial. Ask for special breaks and weekend rates.

Blockley
🆂🆒 🧍 🐕 ▭ **££**

Lower Farm Cottages, *Lower Farmhouse, Blockley, Moreton-in-Marsh, Glos GL56 9DP*
Tel: 0386 700237
Open all year
As you approach Blockley on B4479 from Bourton-on-the-Hill, Lower Farm Cottages lie at the bottom of the hill beside a stream. Variously named, for example, Ratty's Retreat, Mole's Cottage and, grandest of all, Toad Hall, they are all pleasant, with a well-equipped kitchen, comfortable sitting room and bedrooms freshly decorated in a light, country style. The grounds are compact but well designed so that children have enough open space to play cricket or croquet. There's a tree fort in a pear tree and even a small boat for them to use in the stream. At quiet times you may see a heron or kingfisher on the water.

Broadway
🏠 ✕ 🧍 🐕 ▭ **££££**

The Lygon Arms, *Broadway, Worcs WR12 7DU*
Tel: 0386 852255
Open all year
This restored and extended 16th-century manor house is now a luxury hotel, the most prestigious in the Cotswolds. Bedrooms in the old part of the building have low beamed ceilings, antique oak furniture and impeccable soft furnishings. In the more modern garden and orchard wing the bedrooms are rather bigger, though similarly decorated, with

Autumn Meet at The Lygon Arms

Street, Cotswold House is now an excellent hotel and restaurant run by Gill and Robert Greenstock. The 18th-century classical-style front hall with a fine spiral staircase to the upstairs rooms sets the tone for the rest of the house. There is no hint of corporate uniformity here. The public rooms are elegant and colourful; each bedroom is decorated in its own individual style.

The restaurant (jacket and tie for men), which opens on to a handsome, mature garden, has a high reputation for freshly cooked and inventive dishes. Last orders: Sun lunch 2pm; dinner 9.30pm; Greenstocks, a more casual restaurant attached to the hotel, is open 9.30am-9.30pm.

views of the garden rather than the street. The restaurant, in a great hall complete with minstrel gallery, serves both French *nouvelle cuisine* and traditional English food. Expect to pay about £30 each for dinner. A Country Club is tucked away on two floors in the courtyard area. Use of its floodlit tennis court, 60-foot-long swimming pool, spa bath, sauna, and fitness and billiard rooms is included in the room price.

Chipping Campden
🏠 ✕ ⁒8 ▭ £££

The Cotswold House, *Chipping Campden, Glos GL55 6AN*
Tel: 0386 840330
Open all year; R open for dinner daily & Sun lunch
Formerly a large 17th-century townhouse in the middle of the High

Moreton-in-Marsh
🚗 ⅋ 🐎 ⊠ £

New Farm, *Dorn, Moreton-in-Marsh, Glos GL56 9NS*
Tel: 0608 50782
Open all year except Christmas Day
A mile out of Moreton-in-Marsh on the A427 to Stratford, take the left turning signposted to Dorn. New Farm is first on the right. Mrs Catherine Righton has three double bedrooms, two with bathrooms, all with TV, hand basins, and tea- and coffee-making facilities. The bedrooms are spacious, full of rather heavy but comfortable Victorian furniture and thick pile carpets. There is an equally roomy residents' lounge and dining room downstairs. A three-course evening meal (£8 a head) can be provided with sufficient notice.

WHERE TO EAT

Chipping Campden
✕ ▭ ££

Alexiou's Greek Tavern, *High Street, Chipping Campden*
Tel: 0386 840826
Closed Sun
People come to pass the evening here, not just to eat. The food is good and very reasonably priced. The most popular dish is *meze* which includes hot and cold *hors d'oeuvres* and a barbecue platter of pork, chicken, lamb and beef. There is a distinctly Mediterranean ambience despite the fireplaces and the Cotswold stone; waiters, most of them Greek, may sing and diners may dance if the mood takes them, as it often does. The front of the restaurant looks out on the High Street and in summer the doors are open onto the patio garden at the back. Last orders for dinner: 11pm.

Chipping Campden
🏠 ✕ ▭ £££

The Vinery Restaurant, *Seymour House Hotel, High Street, Chipping Campden*
Tel: 0386 840429
Open all year
Well named, because the main feature of this restaurant is the mature vine growing in the middle of the restaurant (formerly a courtyard) towards a low skylight. The management of both hotel and restaurant is Italian and, not surprisingly, the speciality here is Italian food. A typical three-course dinner might consist of a starter of risotto with quails, followed by a classic *ossobucco milanese* and an *amaretto crème brûlée* to finish.

The decor is stylish in pink and green; the atmosphere intimate. Last orders: lunch 2pm; dinner 9.45pm.

Moreton-in-Marsh
✕ ▭ £££

Annies Restaurant, *Moreton-in-Marsh*
Tel: 0608 51981
Closed 2 wks end Jan/beg Feb & Sun eve
This restaurant, housed in a 300-year-old traditional Cotswold building, with stone flags, beamed ceilings, and three fireplaces, is run by David and Anne Ellis. It is well-known and loved in these parts for the food - described as 'English and French country cooking' - and for the welcoming atmosphere. Last orders: lunch 2pm; dinner 10pm.

Moreton-in-Marsh
✕ ▭ £££

The Marsh Goose, *High Street, Moreton-in-Marsh*
Tel: 0608 52111
Closed Sun eve & Mon
Set in what was once the stables for the Georgian house next door (now Lloyds Bank), The Marsh Goose is an elegant and much praised restaurant, cleverly divided into separate dining areas, with a connecting lounge built on the site of the original stable yard. Expect to pay about £19 for a starter of spinach and Parma ham tart followed by roast partridge with puréed root vegetables in a red wine and parsley sauce, and a pudding of chocolate roulade on raisin shortbread. The wine list is strong on dessert wines. Last orders: lunch 2pm; dinner 9.30pm.

THE EASTERN WOLDS

The eastern Cotswolds descend from their highest point in Stow-on-the-Wold to the open country of the Evenlode valley and the Oxfordshire wolds. The river Windrush forms a natural boundary to the south and a Roman road, the Fosse Way, slants up between the ancient towns of Stow-on-the-Wold and Northleach forming a boundary to the west. It's an interesting stretch of countryside, encompassing quietly perfect villages and more mainstream tourist attractions.

Families with children, for instance, are guaranteed a variety of attractions at Bourton-on-the-Water and, close by, there's Folly Farm with its wildfowl lakes and deer and donkeys. If the weather looks threatening, the recently bypassed Northleach has two excellent museums. The towns of Burford and Stow-on-the-Wold are both busy beauty spots, with an ancient history and enough shops and restaurants to divert the keenest consumer. Famously picturesque villages like the Slaughters and the Swells have their fans but for equally lovely though lesser known Cotswold villages follow the suggested circular drive from Stow-on-the-Wold. This part of the Cotswolds is ideal for walkers and all tourist information offices stock general walking guides as well as leaflets giving their own local suggestions.

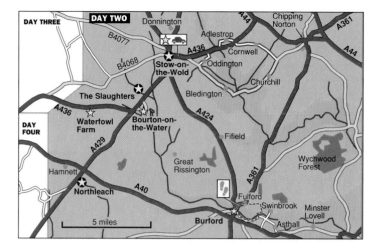

☆ BOURTON-ON-THE-WATER

People often call Bourton-on-the-Water 'Blackpool of the Cotswolds', a snide reference to the cheerful, knees-up atmosphere that pervades the town on a hot summer's day. Bourton's other name, 'Venice of the Cotswolds', hardly tells the whole truth either, despite the presence of the river and its dinky bridges beside the main street. But Bourton-on-the-Water is different from other Cotswold towns. Aside from the usual shops, cafés, restaurants, there is also a Model Village (of Bourton), and the Birdland park and the Motor Museum, all commercial attractions and all, in their own way, entertaining.

The **Model Village**, tucked away in the back garden of the Old New Inn, opened in 1937 and is the town's oldest purpose-built attraction. The houses, river and bridges are all there on a 1:9 scale, large enough to be interesting. Piped hymn music issues from the model of Bourton Baptist church and there is, of course, a model of the model village in the model of the Old New Inn yard.

Opening times: daily 9am-6.45pm
Admission: adult £1.20; child 90p

Further along the High Street, the **Model Railway Exhibition** is a sure winner for some, deeply boring for others. There are over 40 trains for visitors to propel over three main displays, with tracks through mountains, around lakes and over bridges. Space is limited and you may have to fight for your share of the controls. The attached model and toy shop attracts real enthusiasts.

Opening times: daily Apr-Sept 11am-5.30pm; weekends only Oct-Mar 11am-5pm. Admission: adult £1.25; child £1

Cotswold Motor Museum, Bourton-on-the-Water

Across the High Street on a bend of the river, the **Cotswold Motor Museum** is housed in a former 18th-century water mill. In fact, it is a collection of virtually anything that ever moved on wheels, including vintage bicycles, toys, old prams, 1920s caravans and ancient two-wheeled roller skates, as well as motorbikes and cars. Brum, the vintage car character from the BBC children's series of the same name, lives here and sets off on his adventures from this very museum. Children come to pay their respects.

The **Village Life Exhibition**, in another part of the building, re-creates an old shop, a forge and a kitchen from earlier this century; a dusty clutter of tin advertising signs (the country's largest collection on public display) mangles and sewing machines all look rather messy at first. Get your eye in and the detail soon proves interesting.

The Exhibition is a timely reminder that before World War II less than a quarter of all the cottages in the Cotswolds had electricity and only four out of every hundred had inside bathrooms. In fact, rural poverty was only mitigated by the welfare state and the growth of tourism, the arrival of young, affluent weekenders and older people retiring to the countryside.

Opening times for both museums: daily Feb-Nov 10am-6pm
Admission: adult £1.20; child 60p

The **Cotswold Perfumery** in the centre of the village is hardly worth the admission charge, offering a dull audio-visual show on the history of perfume-making and a walk into a tiny patch of perfume garden to see some perfectly ordinary garden plants. You can purchase the house perfumes, gifts and trinkets in the shop attached to the perfumery which is open every day.

A couple of minutes' walk away at the other end of the village, the three-acre park of **Birdland** runs along a river, teeming with both fish and fowl. It was the brainchild of entrepreneur Len Hill who once bought two Falkland islands to preserve their population of penguins. Predictably, a great attraction here is the colonies of portly looking King Penguins and Falklands Kelp Geese, brought as eggs from South Georgia island and hatched and reared in this country.

These are among 600-odd species of birds which also include exotic Amazon parrots, African hornbills and golden crested cranes. Free-flying birds are a delight. Parrots and cockatoos sidle towards the visitor hoping to be fed, and they're rarely disappointed. The fish get fed too. Trout, of golden, grey and rainbow varieties, swim fat and contented in the narrow river. They are offered for sale, fresh or smoked, as you leave.

Opening times: daily all year - Apr-Oct 10am-6pm; Nov-Mar 10am-4pm
Admission: adult £3; child £2

If you ask any local the best place for lunch in these parts, **The Lamb** at **Great Rissington** is likely to be top of their, admittedly, long list. A picturesque inn in the centre of the village, it serves bar meals at lunchtime, including home-made steak pie, and the restaurant is open in the evening. There is a delightful, peaceful garden at the back with views of the village below. A lovely place to sit out in the summer, sip Wadworth 6X or Hook Norton Best, and contemplate how well the garden has come on since the bomber nose-dived it during the war.

☆ BURFORD

The lovely broad street of Burford climbs gently at first, then more steeply to the top of a hill. At the bottom, the town's boundary is marked by the green and willowy River Windrush, spanned by the sweetest mediaeval stone bridge. In between run a higgledy-piggledy jumble of roofscapes: shops, houses and hotels in stone and timber-framed buildings of the mid-15th to 18th centuries.

The town is much given over to antique shops these days. But it always was quick to seize on a commercial opportunity: in the Middle Ages, it was an important market town; then a centre for saddlery (both Charles II and William of Orange received gifts of saddles); a source of the best stone for miles (some Oxford colleges, Blenheim Palace and parts of London, after the Great Fire of 1666, were built from Burford stone); and also a culinary centre (usually involving venison poached from surrounding Wychwood forest).

Start your exploration of the town at the **Tolsey**, on the corner of High Street and Sheep Street. This was the original meeting place (from about 1500) of the burgesses who set and collected the toll charges for the town's markets and fairs. It is now a small museum with a collection of ancient local seals and charters which may prove more interesting to the specialist than the general tourist. However, the staff are great enthusiasts of local history and happy to share their knowledge. Small markets take place every day beneath the Tolsey arcades – the Women's Institute on Fridays.

Burford High Street

(i) Continue along Sheep Street and call in at the **Tourist Information Centre** (tel: 0993 823558), tucked into the back room of an old brewery, for a map and guide to the town. Further on, the **Bay Tree Hotel** is said to be the birthplace of Sir Lawrence Tanfield, an important local hate-figure from the 17th century.

When he bought the lordship of the manor, he began repossessing ancient rights which had been enjoyed for years by the town's burgesses. In the process he became so heartily disliked that when he died in 1625, he had to be buried secretly - at midnight. The town's Mayday celebrations have traditionally included the burning of his effigy.

The Lamb Inn in Sheep Street, reckoned to be the oldest in town with parts dating from the 15th century, is a cosy refreshment stop (see Where to Stay). As you turn right down Priory Lane, the 16th-century priory is on your left - closed to the public but still in use by a mixed community. Down by the river, across the main road, there is a nucleus of ancient buildings (to be admired from the outside), including the late 16th-century Weavers' Cottages, the Grammar School of the same period not far away in Church Street and, beside the church, the Almshouses, built in 1457 by Richard, Earl of Warwick.

The true repository of Burford history is **St John Baptist Church**, built in a mixture of Norman, Early English and Perpendicular styles. The lead font, now covered in a thick sheet of glass, has the words 'Anthony Sedley prisner' scored on its surface for those sharp-eyed enough to distinguish it. Sedley was a disaffected soldier among the radical group of Levellers in Cromwell's army. On 14th May 1649 they were rounded up by Cromwell and held in Burford church. Three soldiers were picked out randomly and shot. Anthony Sedley was not among them.

You can see the plaque marking this event on the outside wall of the Lady Chapel. It was placed there in 1979 by the Workers' Educational Association and unveiled by the Labour politician Tony Benn. Each year the Association gathers to commemorate the event, causing a few tight lips in this conservative town.

In 1896, when William Morris complained to the vicar about the way he was restoring Burford church, the vicar is said to have replied, 'The church, sir, is mine and if I choose to, I shall stand on my head in it'. Morris was apparently highly amused by this riposte but nevertheless retired to Broadway Tower to fire off letters of protest. From there, he founded the Society for the Protection of Ancient Buildings or SCRAPE. He loathed the Victorian obsession with scraping off plaster to reveal bare stonework.

BURFORD WALK

For a one-hour walk, leave Burford by Witney Street until you see the footpath sign on the left which takes you beside the river. Cross fields over five stiles, and leave the last by a gate which leads to a tarred road. Follow this for about 200 yards to Widford Mill Farm. Turn left immediately and cross the bridge, then right across the fields keeping **St Oswald's Church** on your left.

This tiny Norman church stands by itself in open countryside, surrounded by a dry stone wall. The door may be stiff, so push hard to enter. Inside, apart from the huge font, the proportions are those of a simple domestic room with stone flags, tiny box pews and faded wall paintings. The church was built on the site of a Roman villa – hence the coloured mosaics on part of the floor. The church was restored in 1904.

Turn left past the church up a streamless valley, Dean Bottom, with woods on either side and climb the stile onto the metalled road at the top. Walk along the high ridge towards Fulbrook. The road brings you out at the end of the village. Continue towards the Burford roundabout and cross the bridge back into Burford.

To extend the walk for another half hour, continue straight across the fields from St Oswald's Church and enter Swinbrook village by **St Mary's Church**. Lichen-covered table tombs stand in the churchyard. The graves of Unity and Nancy Mitford, daughters of Lord Redesdale, lie near the church entrance. Jessica Mitford wrote an account of her eccentric family and their life in Swinbrook in *Hons and Rebels*.

Don't miss the interior of St Mary's. It has a fine Perpendicular window, carved 15th-century choir stalls and the effigies of six members of the Fettiplace family (early squires of Swinbrook) stacked on top of each other in two groups of three, lying on their sides on bent elbows and in full armour. Apparently, it was the only way they could be made to fit into the available space.

From the church, turn right to the Swan Inn beside the river if you need some refreshment. Or go left up the hill, and left again to join the high metalled road to Fulbrook and thence back to Burford.

The Mitford Connection: the charming villages of Swinbrook and neighbouring Asthall (abundant with flowers in summer) were both home at different times to the Mitford family. The Maytime Inn at Asthall (recently under new management) is one of the prettiest in the Cotswolds. While you are in the area, pop into Minster Lovell. This is a village of thatched cottages with the delightful inn, The Old Swan and Mill (see Where to Eat p39) at one end and the romantic ruins of the 14th-century manor house, Minster Lovell Hall, at the other.

☆ FOLLY FARM WATERFOWL

Young children love Folly Farm, a 50-acre site on a high and windy ridge near Bourton-on-the Water for over 150 different breeds of waterfowl, both wild and domestic, including some rare species. From the entrance at the top of the hill, the track takes you past incubator sheds to breeding pens full of chickens, ducks and geese. Cascades of water lead to two lakes, one full of domestic waterfowl (it can sound like bedlam here at feeding time, with the squawking of birds echoing round the hills), and

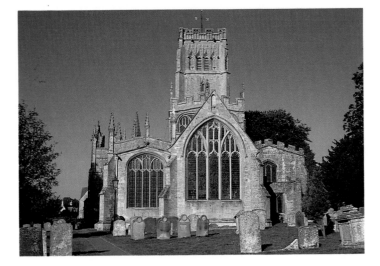

Northleach: Church of St Peter and St Paul

the other reserved for wild waterfowl, virtually empty in the summer. In surrounding fields and enclosures there are colonies of rabbits, goats, sheep, deer and donkeys which, by contrast, are models of peace and quiet.

If you visit between April and the end of June you'll see the new-born chicks. But even later into the year, there are always a few odd eggs being hatched under a hen. There is no lack of opportunity for feeding the animals. Real keenies can adopt a duck.

There is an indoor pet area for children at the top of the hill, housing small animals like guinea pigs, rats and ferrets, a garden centre and a tea room selling home-made cakes and biscuits.

Folly Farm Waterfowl, Folly Farm, Bourton-on-the-Water - signposted from A436. Tel: 0451 20285
Opening times: daily Apr-Sept 10am-6pm; Oct-Mar 10am-3.30pm. The shop stays open an extra hour
Admission: adult £2.70; child £1.60

NORTHLEACH

Most people go to Northleach to visit its church, Keith Harding's World of Mechanical Music or the Countryside Collection just outside the town. The evening attraction is Chris Wickens's restaurant or, for gourmets with fatter wallets, the discreetly expensive Old Woolhouse. Otherwise, with its three-sided market place, its few pubs and shops, the old mills and mill pond and almshouses, Northleach is a quiet town.

The finest building is the **Church of St Peter and St Paul**, just above the market place. This is a veritable cathedral of a church, built in Perpendicular style with profits from the wool trade. It was restored in the 15th century with a high tower and double clerestory windows - all the better to see the memorial brasses of woolmen and their wives. There they are - a brass rubber's dream - the Busshes, the Midwinters, the Forteys, their feet on a sheep or a bag of wool, their chosen epitaphs a model of piety. The modern pews were designed by the architect Sir Basil Spence (1907-76) and made by the craftsmen of Sir Gordon Russell's workshop in Broadway. Locals boast about the fine acoustics of their church which regularly hosts visiting choirs from all over the world.

Northleach: Keith Harding's World of Mechanical Music

Keith Harding's World of Mechanical Music sounds like a side show on a seaside promenade but don't be deceived. This is a top class museum and shop in Northleach High Street, a treasure trove of musical boxes, automata, mechanical musical instruments and antique clocks housed in two rooms of a former merchant's house and grammar school.

The owner, Keith Harding, former monk, father of five and a true enthusiast, repairs automata, clocks and musical boxes sent to him from all over the world. He also exhibits his own stock, including an early long case clock made by John Fowll of London in 1670. Other stock is for sale.

The automata are great fun and full of surprises. A Parisian clown, made in 1770, plays the banjo, a lion tamer tries to make his lion perform tricks but ends up getting eaten. There are pianolas and pianola rolls of Paderewski playing his own minuet from the 1920s and Rachmaninov playing his preludes. Ghosts of the past live on in this museum. The Hardings tell of being woken regularly at night by the sound of the organ beginning to play by itself in the empty house....and you believe them.

The ticket is quite expensive but it includes a one-hour guided tour which is essential. If you're there alone, you'll get a one-person guided tour. Disabled visitors are welcome. Brochures are also printed in braille. The shop, an extension of the museum, sells a mixed collection of children's books, toys and musical toys of an educational nature.

Keith Harding's World of Mechanical Music, Oak House, Northleach. Tel: 0451 60181
Opening times: daily 10am-6pm, except Christmas Day
Admission: adult £3.50; child £1.50; family ticket £8.50

The **Cotswold Countryside Collection** is installed in a rather stately-looking one-time prison just outside Northleach. This is the place to get a flavour both of farming and of prison life in the 19th century. (The connection was perhaps strongest in the 1830s when agricultural labourers who broke up threshing machines were imprisoned here.)

Begin with a tour of the outbuildings around a small open grassed area, formerly the prisoners' exercise yard. The blacksmith's and wheelwright's workshops are interesting if your visit happens to coincide with someone actually demonstrating the work. Otherwise, the display of agricultural tools may be a little arcane for townies. Country themes continue in the main building with audio-visual displays of the history of the ordinary farming people of the area. If you ever entertained romantic views of rural life, prepare to abandon them here. Don't miss the taped recollections of local countryman and writer Fred Archer, recalling his own Gloucester childhood of the 1920s.

In the original cell block (built around 1789), audio-visual effects are used to recreate the drama of trial and sentencing and routine of prison life, not sufficiently dramatic to bring you out in a cold sweat, but interesting, none the less. The courtroom, used well into Victorian times, is now a refreshment area with rather basic offerings of drinks and biscuits. The museum also has a shop and a Tourist Information Office.

Cotswold Countryside Collection, Northleach - access from A429. Tel: 0451 60715
Opening times: daily Apr-Oct 10am-5.30pm, Sun 2-5.30pm
Admission: adult £1; child £0.50

> Victorian vicars were always keen on improving their churches. A mile north-west of Northleach, **St George's Church** at Hampnett had a particularly energetic vicar. He had the interior of his church stencilled in brown, red and green patterns and stuck stars in the wooden ceiling. Purists disapprove but the effect is certainly decorative.

THE SLAUGHTERS (UPPER AND LOWER)

Could it be the attractiveness of these two villages or their curious names (perhaps from Old English 'slough' meaning 'wet ground') that draw tourists here? Whatever the reason, Lower Slaughter is marginally more popular, although many reckon Upper Slaughter is more deserving.

Lower Slaughter spreads itself flat beside the meandering River Eye (a tributary of the Windrush), easy terrain for the elderly folk who have retired here. It's a quiet place. There is an early 19th-century water mill, 17th-century Manor House, now a country hotel, a restaurant with a delightful garden on a bend of the river, a few shops, a church, some council houses, an allotment and a cricket field tucked away out of sight. Not much, considering its popularity. There are easy walks to Stow from here past the cricket pitch and to Bourton-on-the-Water along the Warden's Way by Slaughter Brook. Upper Slaughter is a two-minute drive or a pleasant short walk away.

To walk from Lower Slaughter to Upper Slaughter, take the path between Collett's Bakery and the Post Office. Pass through some kissing gates on to a clear track with the Cotswold Stud on your right and the millpond on your left. Go through a bit of woodland just before you reach the village.

The Lords of the Manor Hotel in Upper Slaughter (once the rectory) is a good place to stop for morning coffee if you've walked across and your shoes aren't too muddy. The Norman church, restored in the 19th century, with a spiky pinnacled tower - rather grand for such a small church - stands on a rise at the edge of a three-sided green. The stone cottages around the green were remodelled by the architect Sir Edwin Lutyens in 1906. The River Eye runs in a shallow stream in a hollow behind the church.

Picturesque Lower Slaughter on the River Eye

The most picturesque brewery in England, that of **Donnington's Ales**, is to be found a mile west of the village of Donnington in a wooded valley beside a mill pond, a source of the river Dikler. A small family brewery, famous throughout the Cotswolds, its buildings are closed to the public, but make an interesting diversion none the less. The village of Donnington saw the surrender of 3,000 Royalist soldiers in the last engagement of the English Civil War on March 21 1646.

✪ STOW-ON-THE-WOLD

It was the lucky convergence of roads which made this town a commercial centre in the 12th century and has kept it so ever since. Never mind that it was on the highest point of the wolds, 'where the wind blows cold', the land was poor and there was no water. There were always sheep, so there was a market. According to Daniel Defoe there were 70,000 sheep for sale at a Stow fair of 1724.

Market Square is full of cars rather than sheep now, but it is still attractive. On one side, a small grassed area, much reduced over the years, carries the 19th-century village stocks, and on another stands the mediaeval market cross (with Victorian headstone). The narrowest streets which lead into the square are the original sheep runs, or tures. The buildings around the square, now hotels, or antique and interior design shops, are from the 17th and 18th century. The architectural horror is the Gothic-style Assembly rooms, St Edward's Hall, dumped right in the middle of the square by the Victorians. It must have destroyed a fine sense of spaciousness, but it is part of the scenery now.

Stow, with its Market Square and busy Sheep Street, has a more ample, roomy feel to it than other Cotswold towns which are built around a single main street. It still has two horse fairs a year, but its main business is undoubtedly year-round tourism supported by good class hotels and shops. New shopping precincts have been the butt of disparaging remarks about the 'gentrification' of the Cotswolds. And there are those who complain that Stow has been so polished up for the tourists that locals hardly feel they belong. But you can't deny it's very pretty.

Stow: Hotel on Market Square

One of the many antique shops

Lillian Middleton is a well known doll maker with premises in Sheep Street. Her dolls are rather special - handmade (using traditional 19th-century German methods), designer dressed (she was a couturier) and much sought after. One of the most popular is the Queen Mother doll. Orders take about six weeks to complete and cost anything from £30-£300.

Visit the quiet churchyard of **St Edward** just behind the square, with pigeons cooing among dark yew trees. The church itself has mediaeval origins although you would not guess it. The restoration it underwent after Royalist troops were imprisoned here during the Civil War and further 19th-century rebuilding have not improved it. Before fear of vandals closed the church tower (what happened to gentrification?) it was possible to climb it and choose your walking route from the top. Now, it's better just to visit the very helpful **Tourist Information Centre** in Stow (tel: 0451 31082) and pick up some suggested trails.

☆ A VILLAGE DRIVE

This is a circular, 20-mile drive from Stow-on-the-Wold through some smaller villages of interest in the north-eastern Cotswolds.

From Stow take the A436 eastwards for about three miles and turn left into **Adlestrop**. The village is immortalised in a poem by Edward Thomas familiar to every British schoolchild, at least of an earlier generation, which begins:

'Yes. I remember Adlestrop -

The name, because one afternoon

Of heat the express-train drew up there

Unwontedly. It was late June.'

The railway sign Thomas gazed at is now displayed on the back wall of the bus shelter which you pass as you drive through the village. Rejoin the A436, turn left and almost immediately right into an unmarked road and then follow signs to **Cornwell**. This village was bought in a state of decay by a wealthy American woman just before the Second World War and completely re-created by the Welsh architect Clough Williams-Ellis (who also transformed the village of Portmeirion in Wales). The manor house and gardens are private property but you can catch a tantalising glimpse of them as you drive past.

Continue for a couple of miles until you get to the B4450. (Look left for a brief sight of the town of Chipping Norton and the tall towers of the Victorian Bliss Tweed Mill, now luxury apartments.) Turn right here to **Churchill**, where a huge Victorian church and bizarre gothic fountain guard the village green. Continue out of town for about four miles, cross a railway bridge and turn right into the village of **Bledington**. The Bledington dances, a variety of Morris dancing, take place here on the green and in the courtyard of the Bledington Arms on Sundays from May to September.

Leave Bledington by the B4450 Stow road and continue for several miles until you reach a right turn to Upper Oddington (the Horse and Groom is a good pub stop). Drive through to **Lower Oddington**, where a sign by the post office on the right points to St Nicholas Church, half a mile away. The 11th-century church is charming, both in itself and its location, but more remarkable for its 14th-century doom painting along one wall. The sight of sinners hanging by their necks and being boiled alive while the virtuous are helped up the walls of the City of Heaven by saints and angels must once have been the equivalent of a short, sharp shock. Return to the village, turn right at the post office and join the A436 back to Stow-on-the-Wold.

WHERE TO STAY

Burford
Ꮔ ⅄ ⋊ ⋈ ££

Bee Cottage, *Waterloo Farm Gate, Fulbrook, Oxon OX18 4BZ*
Tel: 0993 822070
Open all year
Jane and Scott McGuire's cottage is on a corner of a farm entrance on the main Fulbrook road: a rural setting, where water comes from a natural spring. Guest accommodation is a spacious two-person suite in a self-contained annexe. There is a bedroom with shower and a private sitting room with colour TV and tea- and coffee-making facilities. Both are fully carpeted and comfortably furnished. Breakfast is served in the privacy of your sitting room: You have your own key and come and go as you wish.

Burford
⋒ ⅄ ⋊ ▭ £££

The Lamb Inn, *Sheep Street, Burford, Oxon OX8 4LR*
Tel: 099382 3155
Open all year
The oldest inn in Burford - and it looks it, too, though most agreeably. It's like being in a private house. The reception desk is in an enclosed little snug in a corner of the lounge. There are flowers on the table, high settles

and open fireplaces, stone floors and window seats. The hotel has 15 individually decorated bedrooms, each with bathroom, tucked in above creaky stairs and reached by labyrinthine passages. The newer bedrooms of the extension are spacious and bright. The garden is particularly lovely with flowers round a quiet rectangle of lawn, contained on one side by the old stone wall of the brewery next door.

Lower Swell
꒱ ⅄ ⋊ ▭ £££

Sunnyside Cottage, *Lower Swell. Rent from Rural Retreats, Blockley, Moreton-in-Marsh, Glos GL56 9DZ.*
Tel: 0386 701177
Open all year
Sunnyside Cottage, in the centre of the village of Lower Swell, is owned and managed by Rural Retreats which aims to let houses which could almost rank as country house hotels. So, all the linen is high quality, the welcome basket includes a good bottle of wine, the furniture is often antique, and the rooms are beautifully decorated. There are four bedrooms, two staircases (this was once two houses), a bathroom and a shower room, reception rooms and facilities including stereo, dishwash-

er etc. Although you are in the centre of the village, the garden is well planted to make you feel secluded. You can book in on any day of the week for a minimum of two nights. Your booking entitles you to automatic membership of Radbrook Manor Country Club near Stratford, which includes use of pool, Jacuzzi, solarium, squash and tennis courts.

Northleach
ⓖ 🐴 🖃 ££

Prospect Cottage, *West End, Northleach, Glos GL54 3HG*
Tel: 0451 60875
Open all year
Mrs. Hobley has two welcoming double bedrooms in a large, terraced cottage in the centre of Northleach. The whole house has been recently done up so that it might be better described now as a modern house with period details (huge exposed beams and stone walls) in the shell of a 300-year old cottage. Each room is on a different floor with its own spacious, tiled bathroom and shower. The bedrooms are well decorated in cottage style with good furniture and

matching duvet covers, headboard and curtains. There is colour TV and a hospitality tray in each room. A comfortable guest sitting room also serves as a breakfast room.

Stow-on-the-Wold
ⓖ 🏃 🐴 🖂 ££

Bretton House, *Fosseway, Stow-on-the-Wold, Glos GL54 1JU*
Tel: 0451 30388
Open all year
Bretton House is a substantial former Edwardian rectory on the A429 just south of Stow-on-the-Wold. It is set well back from the road in a large garden with fine views. The three double bedrooms, with good-sized adjoining bathrooms, are extremely comfortable and well decorated in Laura Ashley wallpapers and fabrics. Clock radio, colour TV and tea- and coffee-making facilities are provided. The owners, Barry and Julia Allen, are friendly and professional. Barry, a former chef, serves a gourmet three-course meal on request for £12.50. You can bring your own wine.

WHERE TO EAT

Bledington
🏠 🖂 ££

The King's Head Inn and Restaurant, *Bledington, nr Kingham*
Tel: 0608 71365
Open all year
The King's Head Inn beside the green at Bledington is a pub, a restaurant and a hotel - and well used in all instances. The building dates from 1530. The bar is a place of cosy settles and tiny nooks. Rather

more formal, the dining room has pink linen, fresh flowers and candles on the table. Traditional dishes like chitterlings and tripe, oxtail, rabbit and jugged hare are on offer as well as house specialities like roast rack of lamb with fresh rosemary sauce. Expect to pay around £16 for a three-course meal. Bar snacks are also available. Last orders: lunch 2pm (1.30pm Sun); dinner 9.45pm (10pm Sun).

Fifield

✕ ▭ ££

Merrymouth Inn, *Stow Road, Fifield*
Tel: 0993 831652
Open all year
This cheerful inn on the main A424
between Burford and Stow-on-the-
Wold wins hearty local recommenda-
tions for good value. Run by the
White family, the emphasis here is on
home-cooked food at a reasonable
price. Bar meals of steak and kidney
pie, half a roast chicken and - house
speciality - barbecued spare ribs,
come with chips and salad garnish
for £5. There are always vegetarian
dishes on offer too. From the grill
room, open on Thursday, Friday and
Saturday, you have a choice of steak,
chicken, venison or local trout
cooked on an open log grill.
Merrymouth also has nine bedrooms
with bathrooms. £42 per room, b&b.
Last orders: lunch 2pm; dinner
9.30pm.

Minster Lovell

⌂ ✕ ▭ ££££

The Old Swan Restaurant, *The Old
Swan and Mill, Minster Lovell*
Tel: 0993 774441
Open all year
The Old Swan is a recently refurbished 600-year-old inn in a stone
and thatch village beside the
Windrush. The restaurant, lofty with
exposed rafters and beams, solid oak
furniture and wooden floor, is ele-
gantly rustic. The atmosphere is calm

but not hushed. The *table d'hôte* menu
is brief and the food is excellent. For
those who want to eat lightly at mid-
day lunch can be a one-, two- or
three-course meal ranging from £9.50
to £13.50. Accommodation at the inn
is luxurious. The adjoining Old Mill
hotel and conference centre is under
the same management.

Northleach

✕ ▭ ££

Wickens, *Market Place, Northleach*
Tel: 0451 60421
*Open all year: lunch daily; dinner Tues-
Sat*
Christopher and Joanna Wickens
specialise in modern English cooking
which means fresh ingredients
(preferably local) freshly cooked, and
a light touch with traditional dishes.
Eliza Acton's recipe for spiced beef
with some modifications, for
instance, is a favourite. Joanna's
sticky toffee pudding and Italian-
style *semi-freddo*, or iced mousse, are
always popular. Wine is mainly from
English-speaking countries -
Australia, New Zealand, South
Africa, the US and England - with
some top-of-the-range French wine at
top prices. The service is prompt and
friendly, the decor is unfussy - white
walls, beamed ceilings, plain furniture and plain white linen. There is
one main dining area which over-
flows into a most attractive conservatory. Last orders: lunch 1.45pm; dinner 8.30pm.

CHELTENHAM
AND THE WEST

The Cotswold escarpment from Broadway to Cheltenham falls steeply westwards to the Vale of Evesham. Bredon Hill, to the north-west, is still considered part of the Cotswold Area of Outstanding Natural Beauty although the open aspect of sur-rounding villages, and their mixed timber and stone houses, reveal it as belonging in equal parts to the flatter vale and the hillier wold.

To the east, it's a different matter. Stone-built villages like Stanton, Stanway and Guiting Power lie folded under hills, their houses typically Cotswold - steep, many-gabled roofs topped by ball finials, their slates progressively wider and curving out-wards as they descend. William Morris said they gave him 'the same sort of pleasure in their orderly beauty as a fish's scales or a bird's feathers'. The golden limestone is porous and must throw off the rain speedily if it is not to become water-logged. You will notice that the decorative, projecting mouldings on many of the stone mullioned windows also keep the rain off.

From the best of Cotswold vernacular to the best of Regency: Cheltenham, spa town and western gateway to the Cotswolds, offers all the pleasures of a snappy modern town, including fine restaurants, shops and a theatre. Energetic young people will enjoy the entertainments of Pittville Park right in Cheltenham with its boating lake and leisure centre. Sudeley Castle, near

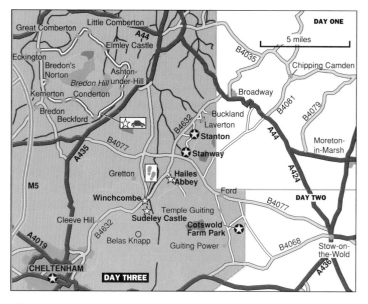

Winchcombe, also has a range of weekend outdoor entertainment plus the best adventure playground for miles. This is great walking country if you're feeling fit; otherwise let the steam train take the strain between Toddington and Winchcombe, or drive round Bredon Hill and check out the modern Arts and Crafts enterprises that continue in the spirit of the original movement. If you have a choice, go in springtime when the orchards of the Vale of Evesham are snowy with blossom.

Typical Cotswolds dry stone walling

☆ BREDON HILL DRIVE

This 18-mile circuit encompasses the small villages around the foot of Bredon Hill on the western edge of the Cotswolds. With their black and white timber frame houses, orchards and vegetable fields, they belong to a different architectural and farming tradition from the rest of the Cotswolds. But the craft tradition, particularly pottery and silk screen printing, remains as strong here as anywhere.

Begin at Beckford, following an anti-clockwise route signposted to Grafton, passing through the villages of Ashton-under-Hill, Elmley Castle, Little Comberton, Great Comberton, Eckington, Bredon, Kemerton, Overbury, Conderton and back to Beckford.

Beckford Silk has new premises, clearly signed, just outside the village, where they print, paint and make up silk ties, shirts and scarves. Visitors are welcome in both shop and workshop. There is also a small, licensed cafe which serves delicious home-made food (closed Sunday). Ashton-under-Hill, the next substantial village, has been described as being close to the fictional Ambridge of the BBC radio serial *The Archers*. You may spot Jill and Phil in the local pub. Little Comberton and Great Comberton, which has the largest dovecote in England, are in the middle of fruit-growing country, fragrant with blossom in spring.

Elaine Rippon's silk shop and studio, Conderton

From Eckington, the road leads to **Bredon** where you will find a
14th-century tithe barn owned by the National Trust; then
Overbury, with a fine 18th-century manor house; then to the pottery at **Conderton**. Here, too, you can watch work in progress
and visit the showroom (closed Sunday). If you are the sort of
person who buys silk waistcoats from Liberty's, you could cut
out the middle man and buy them straight from Elaine Rippon's
studio and shop on the opposite side of the street. She and her
husband paint and print silk in bright, bold, modern designs.
Ponder your choice over a slice of home-made cake and cappuc-
cino coffee in their light and airy coffee shop. They close Sunday
and Monday and from January to March.

The **Yew Tree** pub in Conderton, just across the road from the
silk workshop, is painted pink, in contrast to everything else
around here which is painted green - on the instructions of the
large private estate which owns most of the land. 'It's getting a
bit better now but we used to be the only people in the country
with green telephone boxes,' says a local with a nod in the direction of the manor house in Overbury. The Yew Tree, being free-
hold, can be as pink as it likes. The food here is standard pub
fare but the welcome is warm and the locals are friendly.

CHELTENHAM

This elegant spa town, western gateway to the Cotswolds, has
George III to thank for its fortunes. In 1788 he spent five weeks
there taking the waters. They didn't do him the slightest good,
but armed with this seal of royal approval, the town has never
looked back. Its fashionable status and wealth produced fine
Regency architecture, crescents and squares, parks and gardens.

Modern-day residents, many employed in the defence industry
or by the large insurance companies based around Cheltenham,
are a rather different breed from the old servants of empire who
once retired here for their health. Under this new patronage, the
town has become a true cultural, gastronomic and fashion
mecca.

The **Tourist Information Centre** in the wide chestnut-lined
Promenade (tel: 0242 522878) gives all the guidance you will

need for exploring, including maps and suggestions for town walks. The Promenade itself is a Regency showcase, laid out in 1817 for the use of subscribers only and barred to servants and dogs. Now we can all go strolling up to the Imperial Gardens and Queen's Hotel and into Montpellier Walk, admiring the classical façades and the delicate wrought-iron balconies. Here, you will find a much photographed Cheltenham feature: stone caryatids, classical female figures, separating the buildings; and here too, in this small Montpellier nucleus, are some of Cheltenham's smartest shops.

Cheltenham is known for its top-notch **fashion shops**. Kimberley and Christopher Barry, under the same management and both on Montpellier Arcade, specialise in Italian fashion and accessories for men and women. Alison Harrison at the Courtyard, Montpellier, stocks clothes by top designers including Nicole Farhi, Georges Rech, Nic Janik and Strenesse. Next door, Pragnell sell shoes by French designers Robert Clergerie and René Caty ranging in price from £129 to 'no more than £300' a pair. Tights come from Italy and costume jewellery from New York. Cocoa at Queens Circus specialises in antique lace, particularly for brides. Scott Cooper in the Promenade sells top drawer jewellery - the sort that dare not speak its price, at least in the window.

The elegant Regency Promenade, Cheltenham

Cheltenham verandahs

Back in the centre of town, the **Cheltenham Art Gallery and Museum** has a collection of Dutch and British painting from the 17th century to the present day and an Oriental Gallery with some good Chinese pottery and costumes. The most impressive collection is the work of the Arts and Crafts movement. Of particular note are the walnut table with inlaid ebony and holly by Gimson and Voysey, and jewellery and silverwork designed by C R Ashbee and George Hart of Chipping Campden. The small museum café serves light meals freshly made.

Cheltenham Art Gallery and Museum, Clarence Street, Cheltenham. Tel: 0242 237431
Opening times: Mon-Sat 10am-5.20pm; May 1-Sept 30 also Sun 2-5.20pm
Admission: free

Leaving the Gallery, turn left and follow the inner ring road down North Street, and continue northwards until you reach the iron gates leading to **Pittville Estate**, a park of villas, gardens, ornamental lakes and bridges - another great nucleus of Regency architecture. This is where everybody congregates on summer afternoons between May and September - 'the season' in Cheltenham. On Sundays, there's music from the bandstand, and carriage rides on old-fashioned landaus through the park or through Regency Cheltenham. Across the Evesham road, there's also a boating lake and sports centre; continuing north, you soon come to Cheltenham racecourse, home, each spring, of the Gold Cup meeting.

The classical domed **Pittville Pump Room and Museum** stands on a rise at the north end of the park. The pump still produces spa water (warm, salty and flat) and people still bring their empty plastic bottles to fill up here. On Sundays, the Great Hall is open for late breakfast, lunch and tea, all to the accompaniment of live music from a chamber ensemble or a brass band. Then the Pump Room recaptures some of that sense of gaiety one imagines from the Regency period when it was known as 'the merriest sick resort on earth'. The Museum on the first floor, attended by cheerful and knowledgeable staff, has a costume collection from the 1700s to the 1960s (not a patch on Bath's) and Georgian and Victorian jewellery.

Pittville Pump Room and Museum, Pittville Park. Tel: 0242 512740
Opening times: Nov-Mar, Tues-Sat 10.30am-5pm; Apr-Oct, Tues-Sun 10.30am-5pm
Admission: adult 55p; child 30p

Gustav Holst Birthplace Museum by the town entrance to Pittville Estate is where the composer was born in 1874 and lived for a few years as a child. His grand piano, displayed in the sitting room, is one of the few pieces of Holst memorabilia in the house. The rooms are rather perfunctorily furnished and decorated in late Regency and Victorian style - the stuff of dull school outings. They could liven it up by playing some Holst music through the house.

Gustav Holst Birthplace Museum, 4 Clarence Road, Pittville. Tel: 0242 524846
Opening times: Tues-Fri noon-5.20pm & Sat 11am-5.20pm
Admission: free

A **steam train** runs between Toddington and Winchcombe on summer weekends, passing through Didbrook and Hailes. It used to be part of the Great Western Railway but it is now run by volunteers of the Gloucestershire Warwickshire Railway. The train leaves Toddington on the hour between 11am and 5pm. It stops briefly at Greet, a mile's roadside walk from Winchcombe, then curves round the Cotswold escarpment and through a long tunnel to Gretton (you can't get on or off here) and comes back to pick up any passengers from Greet bound for Toddington at 37 minutes past the hour. If you stay on the train, the whole trip takes about 50 minutes. Call 0242 621405 for information. There are plans to extend the track to Cheltenham and Broadway.

✪ COTSWOLD FARM PARK

If the phrase 'endangered species' makes you think of Brazilian rainforests or African savannahs, take a trip into the rolling Cotswold uplands near Guiting Power. Here, in 25 acres of high pastureland, Joe Henson and John Neeve began their work of conserving rare farm breeds in 1970.

Among these fields, once quarried for stone - hence their dips and hollows - you can see the original Cotswold Lion sheep (so-called for the thick fleece over their foreheads) which brought such wealth to the Cotswolds. Gloucester Old Spot pigs (much in demand as extras in period films) have been successfully crossed with a wild boar resulting in 'tame' wild boar. There are long-horned cattle, sheep with four horns and tiny miniature sheep from a North Atlantic island, reckoned to be close to those bred by Stone Age Man.

Apart from the exotic breeds, there are Exmoor ponies and shire horses as well as farmyard pigs and goats and, in their own sea-son, piglets, chicks and ducklings. You'd think a Pet's Corner would be redundant in these circumstances but children love it. The spring and autumn lambing season - round April/May and the second half of September - is a lively time to call. Summer visitors can see sheep shearing from the Spring Bank Holiday weekend to the middle of June, and each weekend there are demonstrations of country crafts like blacksmithing, woodwork-ing and bee-keeping. There is a small playground and picnic area, a shop and a café which serves snacks. Bank Holidays are always busy. The quietest time to visit is Saturday morning.

Cotswold Farm Park, Bemborough Farm, nr Guiting Power - signposted from B4077 Stow/Tewkesbury Road. Tel: 0451 850307
Opening times: Good Fri or 1st weekend Apr (whichever is earlier)-last weekend Sept, daily 10.30am-6pm
Admission: adult £2.80; child £1.25

The Plough Inn at Ford serves standard bar food and restaurant meals (very generous portions) and the local Donnington ale. A rather indifferent exterior conceals a welcoming interior with flag floors, wooden settles, rough stone walls, darts and shove ha'penny. It is famous for its early asparagus from the Vale of Evesham. Open all day from 9am. Breakfast served from 10am. Last orders: lunch 2.15pm; dinner 9.15pm.

☆   HAILES ABBEY

This was once a great Cistercian abbey, surrounded by hills full
of sheep and vineyards. Now only rooks caw among the tall
chestnut trees that mark its boundaries and its foundations and
cloister arches stand open to the sky. Founded in 1246 by
Richard, Duke of Cornwall, it was grand enough then, but grew
even more splendid after Richard's son Edmund gave the abbey
a phial of the blood of Christ. Hailes became a major shrine for
pilgrims from all over Europe, and its community one of the
wealthiest in the land. With the dissolution of the monasteries in
the 16th century, the abbey was disbanded. The stone was carried away to build houses at Winchcombe and the blood of
Christ was declared to be nothing more than 'honey clarified and
coloured with saffron'.

The ruins are wonderfully atmospheric but don't neglect the
museum. The original 13th-century vaulting bosses, the decorative meeting point of the ribs of the roof arches, are particularly
beautiful. How they escaped being used as Winchcombe
doorsteps is a stunning mystery.

Hailes Abbey, Stanway - access from A46 Opening times: Good Fri-end Sept daily
10am-1pm & 2-6pm; rest of year Tues-Sun 10am-1pm & 2-4pm; closed Dec 24-26
Admission: adult £1.60; child 80p

The ruins of Hailes Abbey

Opposite the abbey is a tiny 12th-century church, backing on to fields, which has simple wooden boxed pews, a carved rood screen and the most delightful mediaeval wall painting. The lines and colours are faded as though some energetic child with a rubber has been hard at work on it, but you can make out St Christopher carrying the Christ-child and patches of a hunting scene. Hounds chase a hare that sits startled beneath a tree, almost as though he had just been wakened out of sleep. This is a sweetly devotional place and a perfect counterpoint to the lost grandeur of the ruins nearby.

> **Hales Fruit Farm** sell their own soft fruit (pick-your-own) and cob nuts (their speciality) and produce their own cider. They are enthusiastic propagandists of ecological farming - no insecticides or herbicides are used. Children will enjoy the farm trails, accompanied by good natural history notes. The short trail lasts approximately 45 minutes and the longer, $1^{1}/_{2}$ hours.

✪ STANTON AND STANWAY

Together with Buckland and Laverton, Stanton and Stanway form a line of villages immediately below the Cotswold escarpment south of Broadway. They are worth visiting, preferably on foot, because, taken together, they are more quintessentially Cotswold than all the Broadways and Slaughters put together. **Buckland** nestles darkly in wooded hollows. The manor is now a country house hotel and the church has stained glass windows repaired by William Morris. **Laverton** possesses no great architectural treasure but is lovely none the less, although with so many of its houses now weekend homes, it has also become an example of the truly deserted Cotswold village.

Next comes **Stanton**, in ruins until the architect Sir Philip Stott bought it early this century and restored it virtually stone by stone to its (mostly) 17th-century state. He also brought water and electricity to the village. The road between Stanton and Stanway is a long and lovely oak avenue with fields on either side. Just before you reach Stanway, there is a cricket pitch on your right (where the writer J M Barrie often played when he

Thatched cricket pavilion on staddle stones, Stanway

stayed as a house guest at Stanway) with an unusual thatched pavilion raised on staddle stones, like stone mushrooms, above the ground. Visitors to the Cotswolds often have the pleasure of coming upon a game of cricket played on a village green.

Stanway has a Tudor manor house (open some days during the summer), a very fine gabled Jacobean gatehouse, a tithe barn, now used as a village hall, a mediaeval church and, on the edge of the village, a war memorial with St George slaying the dragon. The lettering was done by engraver and sculptor Eric Gill (1882-1940) best known for his carving of Prospero and Ariel on the front of Broadcasting House in London.

☆ SUDELEY CASTLE

This is a castle that has a bit of everything - a few romantic ruins round a substantial mansion, associations of murder, heartbreak and intrigue down the centuries, not to mention an excellent cafeteria, an adventure playground, a craft and garden centre and, on summer weekends, a range of entertainments including jousters, falconry displays and mock battles.

The Parliamentarians ransacked Sudeley during the Civil War and its fortunes only recovered in 1830 when the Dent brothers of Worcester, the great glove-makers of the 19th century, bought and set about restoring it. Their descendants live there now. What we see of the castle today is a rather obvious 19th-century rebuilding of an original 15th-century structure around two large adjacent courtyards. The finest parts of the original building – the hall and the presence chamber – have been left as roofless ruins. Nevertheless, the house has plenty to interest, from fine paintings and furniture to collections of family knick-knacks.

The grounds are attractive, part landscaped parkland and part formal gardens. St Mary's chapel, almost a complete restoration of an original structure from around 1460, houses the tomb and rather romanticised effigy of Catherine Parr under a canopy of angels. Having been widowed by Henry VIII, she married the dreadful and ambitious Thomas Seymour and lived here at Sudeley until she died in childbirth in 1548.

If you are interested in high quality craft work, don't miss the workshops housed in a 15th-century block. Specialists in stained glass, leatherwork and furniture-making produce and sell their work. There is also a permanent exhibition of craft and design with a particularly good lace and needlework collection. Look out for the 18th-century patchwork bag made up of 1,537 pieces. The garden shop sells plants and herbs (open mid-February to Christmas) and the Old Kitchen Restaurant serves good home-made lunches and teas.

Sudeley Castle and Gardens, Winchcombe - access from A46. Tel: 0242 604357
Opening times: daily Easter-Oct noon-5pm; grounds 11am-5.30pm
Admission: adult £4.75; child £2.50; gardens only: adult £3.10; child £1.40
Falconry displays take place Tues, Wednes & Thurs May-Aug. Special outdoor enter-
tainments most summer weekends

Winchcombe Pottery, a mile north of Winchcombe just off the A46, has been a pottery since the beginning of the 19th century. Several potters here specialise in hand-thrown pots produced in a wood-fired kiln. Visitors are welcome to see work in progress when appropriate. The showroom upstairs stocks a variety of domestic pots, mostly good sturdy vessels in the country style, and a running video of the processes. A furniture maker, painter, upholsterer and sculptor also work on the premises. Winchcombe Pottery (tel. 0242 602462) is open Monday-Friday 9am-5pm; Saturday 9am-4pm; Sunday May-September noon-4pm.

☆ WINCHCOMBE

This solid little town on the wooded edge of the Cotswolds has a cheerful, energetic air to it. And although summer visitors tend to treat it as an adjunct to nearby Sudeley Castle, it's worth some time in its own right. Winchcombe was once the capital of the ancient kingdom of Mercia and the site of a great Benedictine Abbey. Nothing much remains of this noble past, but its streets are pleasant, lined with a mixture of stone and black-and-white houses from the 16th century onwards. They are invariably built right to the edge of the pavement, some with steps to the front door.

Visit the restored late 15th-century Perpendicular **Church of St Peter** in the High Street. Its 70 famous fearsome gargoyles leer down at passers-by. Inside, behind protective curtains and glass, is a piece of embroidery said to have been the work of Catherine of Aragon, the Spanish princess and wife of Henry VIII.

Gargoyle on Church of St Peter, Winchcombe

Winchcombe Folk and Police Museum is on the first floor of the Town Hall which also houses an excellent **Tourist Information Centre** (0242 602925), open only in summer. The museum will not be of compelling interest unless it's pouring down outside, or you have a thing about international police uniforms and assorted handcuffs, truncheons and pistols. There is a small entry charge. The seven-holed town stocks outside the building might perhaps suggest a one-time one-legged lag, or was it a case of 'one man one ankle' in Winchcombe?

The Plaisterers Arms on the High Street serves a good pub lunch. It is warm and cosy inside with split level bar and dining area, an outside patio and a garden sloping down to allotments and the River Isbourne at the bottom. A blackboard menu offers standard but well cooked pub food (a starter of fried potato skins with a piquant sauce is the only exotic item) and a traditional roast lunch on Sundays. There are four real ales on offer. Last orders: lunch 2.30pm; dinner 9pm.

The **Railway Museum** on the High Street is a private collection of railway equipment and stock collected by Tim Petchey when the Winchcombe branch line closed in the 1960s. Clustered in his back garden are sleepers, hand-operated signals, railway notices, a booking office with a collection of railway restaurant cutlery, crockery from dining cars and railway uniforms. Children are encouraged to operate signals equipment but they have to fight their dads to do it.

Tobacco plants in this garden may remind you that Winchcombe was a great tobacco-growing area in the 17th century. The crop was later outlawed to protect the Virginian tobacco trade but not without some bloody resistance from the local growers. The small shop sells a useful guide book for 25p as well as tea and biscuits which you can take in the garden.

Winchcombe Railway Museum, 23 Gloucester Street. Tel: 0242 602257
Opening times: daily Easter-end Oct 1.30-6pm; weekends and hols in winter 1.30-dusk
Admission: adult £1.60; child 50p

WINCHCOMBE WALKS

Serious walkers seem to congregate in Winchcombe. If you count yourself among their number you will no doubt have your own plans (consult the Tourist Information Centre if you're stuck). For those who want a gentle potter, there is a very attractive 10-minute walk to Sudeley Castle by way of Vineyard Street, also known as Duck Street after the ducking stool which was the punishment for scolds. Cross the river at the end of the street and follow your nose.

Alternatively, for an hour's stroll to **Belas Knap** neolithic burial site just outside Winchcombe, drive out of town southwards on the Brockhampton Road signposted to Belas Knap. Park in a layby $2^{1}/_{2}$ miles on at another sign. Follow directions up through woodland and round two sides of a field, climbing all the time, to Belas Knap, a great tussocky mound with four burial chambers and an example of 5,000-year old dry stone walling. From the hill there are fine views of Winchcombe town and Sudeley Castle. To walk here from Winchcombe and back, add another hour and a half.

Walkers at Belas Knap

WHERE TO STAY

Cheltenham

🏠 ✕ 🕴 🐴 🍴 ££££

On the Park, *Evesham Road,
Cheltenham, Glos GL52 2AH*
Tel: 0242 518898
Closed 2 wks some time during winter
This hotel, in a fine Regency building
opposite Pittville Park, opened in
1991. The owners, Darryl (late of
Charingworth Manor near Chipping
Campden) and Lesley-Anne
Gregory, have created a very stylish
establishment. Of the eight large and
luxurious bedrooms, two have showers and the rest bathrooms. They are
all decorated differently, with
schemes chosen by Lesley-Anne, an
artist; some plain and elegant, others
floral and flamboyant. Hospitality
trays in the bedrooms include a
decanter of wine, handmade choco-
lates, mineral water plus a handwrit-
ten note of welcome from the
Gregorys. The **Epicurean** restaurant
in the same building is run indepen-
dently by Patrick McDonald who
was also at Charingworth. Hotel
guests on special breaks have meals
included at the Epicurean.

Cheltenham

🏠 🕴 🐴 🍴 ££££

Queen's Hotel, *The Promenade,
Cheltenham, Glos GL52 2AH*
Tel: 0242 514724
Open all year
This hotel, named for Queen Victoria,
belongs solidly in Cheltenham's
grand building tradition. It stands at
the head of the wide Promenade with
views down into the town and
colourful Imperial Gardens. Gilt mirrors, candelabra and comfortable
easy chairs in the lobby set the tone.

The effect is one of ease and comfort
rather than grand style. Bedrooms
are decorated in bold floral patterns
and deep colours: current renova-
tions will retain this Victorian style.
Even if you are not a guest, afternoon
tea at The Queen's is always a treat.
Finger sandwiches, scones with
cream and jam, and freshly made
pastries are served from 3-6pm.

Stanton

🏠 🕴 🐴 ✕ ££

Mrs. Gabb, *Vine Cottage, Stanton,
nr Broadway, Worcs WR12 7NE*
Tel: 0386 73250
Open all year
This guesthouse is ideal for walkers
and riders. Mrs Gabb runs a stable
which looks excellent (adults £10.50
per hour, children £9.50) as well as a
B&B establishment that will appeal
to anyone who likes a cheerful family
atmosphere and doesn't mind a front
hall littered with riding hats. All
rooms (comfortable rather than elegant) have four-poster beds and
showers. One family room sleeps
four. No lunches or evening meals
are provided except for unaccompa-
nied children, usually riders, but the
local pub, The Mount, a short walk
through the village, will feed you.
Their 'Cow Pie' is well known in
these parts.

Stanton

SC 🕴 🐴 🍴 £££

Stanton Court Cottages, *Stanton,
nr Broadway, Worcs WR12 7NE*
Tel: 0386 73551
Open all year
These eight self-catering cottages
have been skilfully converted from

the stables, barns and outbuildings attached to 16th-century Stanton Court. Modern amenities include central heating and telephone, full supply of linen, towels, etc. The large grounds provide a great sense of privacy and space and there is a swimming pool and tennis court for use of guests. Weekly lets are available throughout the year and three-night short breaks in winter.

Winchcombe
ᴳ ⚹ ▭ ££

Sudeley Hill Farm, *Broadway Road, Winchcombe, Cheltenham, Glos GL54 5JA*
Tel: 0242 602344
Open all year except Christmas

Barbara Scudamore looks after the bed and breakfast while her husband runs this 800-acre farm a mile out of Winchcombe, just beyond Sudeley Castle. Parts of the farmhouse date from the 15th century. It stands in a lovely garden with wide views over the fields to Winchcombe. The double, twin and single rooms, all well furnished and decorated, have hand basins and share a large bathroom. The spacious family room, with bathroom, is the only room with a television. There is a comfortable guest sitting room (with TV) and a separate dining room with views of the back garden and the hills beyond, dotted with black Welsh sheep.

WHERE TO EAT

Andoversford
▮ ⋈ ££

The Kilkeney Inn and Brasserie, *Andoversford, nr Cheltenham*
Tel: 0242 820341
R open daily for lunch and dinner except Sun eve in winter

This pub is actually some way west of the village of Andoversford, at the fork where the A436 divides. It was originally a drover's inn and six cottages, now extended into a long bar with a restaurant behind, very cleverly combining the atmosphere of an old-fashioned pub and restaurant. Landlords John and Judy Fennell offer a choice of bar meals and waitress service in the restaurant - a raised conservatory area at the back of the pub with a patio beyond. The menu, identical for lunch and dinner with the addition of cold dishes for lunch, changes weekly. The choice is wide and the prices reasonable. Last orders: lunch 2pm; dinner 9.30pm.

Cheltenham
✕ ▭ ££££

Staithes, *12 Suffolk Road, Cheltenham*
Tel: 0242 260666
Dinner only; closed 1 wk after Christmas
& 2 wks in summer

Chef Paul Lucas started this restaurant in 1991 and it looks set to do extremely well. He took over the premises of an existing restaurant, formerly Redmonds, and gutted and completely revamped it. Walls have been knocked through to create a separate lounge on the first floor for pre- and post-dinner drinks. Smoking is allowed here but not in the dining room. The food is modern English, with generous helpings. You could begin with soup of leek and chives, go on to Scottish salmon served with salmon eggs and champagne sauce and, to follow, individual bread and butter pudding with warm English custard sauce, for around £20. The dining room is elegant in pastel shades of salmon, green and yellow. The restaurant is named after a coastal village in East Yorkshire, home of the British Impressionist movement of painters. Some of their works hang on the walls. Last orders: 10pm. Telephone to book.

Cleeve Hill
✕ ▭ ££££

Redmonds, *Cleeve Hill, Cheltenham*
Tel: 0242 672017
Open all year except for 1 wk after
Christmas: lunch Tues-Fri & Sun; din-
ner Mon-Sat

Redmond and Pippa Hayward are in new premises on Cleeve Hill and their food continues to win plaudits. Try open spinach ravioli with mus-

sels, salmon and mild curry sauce followed by roast best end of lamb in a sweet herb and brioche crumb crust and rosemary. And to crown it all, hot lime soufflé with ginger ice cream. Pippa is in charge of the wine list which is a model of adventurous good sense and good value. House wines are available by the glass or bottle. The decor is simple, warm, and understated, both in the lounge and dining room. Last orders: lunch 2pm; dinner 10pm unless you telephone to make a special request for a later meal. Ring to book anyway. There are also five rooms available (Monday-Saturday) if you're too full to leave at the end of your meal.

Winchcombe
✕ ▭ ££

Pilgrims Bistro, *6 North Street,*
Winchcombe
Tel: 0242 603544
Open all year

Pilgrims Bistro has not long been open in Winchcombe but it has already acquired a reputation for good wholesome food (if you want chips with everything, you'll have to go elsewhere) at a reasonable price. The chef says she serves 'English traditional and European.. oh, and international. Whatever is fresh on the day'. The menu ranges from *osso bucco* to beef in Beamish stout, and sticky toffee pudding to *crème brûlée*. It changes daily and everything is made on the premises. The dining room, formerly part of an old saddlery, is decorated in a mixture of Old Cotswold and Laura Ashley style - white walls, polished wooden floor, and small floral motifs. Last orders: lunch 2pm; dinner 9.30pm.

THE CENTRAL COTSWOLDS

The entire western edge of this middle section of the Cotswolds is high ground, from Devil's Chimney at Leckhampton to Crickley Hill, Birdlip Hill, Coopers Hill, then Painswick and Haresfield Beacons. All along, from what is effectively a single escarpment, there are fine views down towards Gloucester and the Severn Valley. The land stays high as it runs east from here, though now the countryside is broken internally by deep valleys. This is true Cotswold territory. A long straight Roman road, our A417, runs through on its way from Cirencester to Gloucester.

Gloucester itself is not strictly speaking within the Cotswolds, but it's too fine a city to miss out on. An entire day could profitably be spent in Gloucester itself if there weren't so many conflicting demands. Crickley Hill Country Park is a breezy point to look for wild flowers or arrowheads and if the weather continues fine, there are many way-marked trails from here through woods and high, open country. Laurie Lee enthusiasts will certainly wish to visit Slad, his home town, and nearby is the delightful town of Painswick, a magical place in many senses, with a craft centre. There are more crafts at Prinknash Abbey, and if you want a scenic drive - or even two - go up the A46 and down the B4079. Nobody needs reminding that the Cotswolds are full of Roman remains and Chedworth Roman Villa is one of the finest.

DAY FIVE

☆ ## CHEDWORTH ROMAN VILLA

The site of this fourth-century Roman villa lies about a mile north of the village of Chedworth in a sheltered hollow on the edge of Chedworth Woods. What appears at first to be a boy scout camp is revealed as wooden roofs covering three excavated areas round a courtyard. All we see of the superstructure of what was once a two-storey house is a collection of three-feet-high walls. But a glance at the plan soon makes sense of the layout.

This was once a substantial mansion of a farming estate, wealthy enough to import glassware from Germany and oysters from the east coast of England. The dining rooms are well preserved, complete with underfloor central heating, and a mosaic floor with geometric patterned border, the four seasons depicted in each corner. These mosaics were made in Corinium – modern Cirencester. Winter, one of the better preserved, is an old man in a cap with a scarf wrapped warmly round his neck carrying a dead hare in one hand and a stick in the other. If you're convinced that all the Romans ever did was bathe and eat, the National Trust shop and museum/interpretation centre and its nine-minute video will give you a more rounded picture.

Chedworth Roman Villa, nr Yanworth - off A429. Tel: 0242 89256
Opening times: Mar-end Oct, Tues-Sun 10am-5pm; Nov-Dec, Wednes-Sun 11am-4pm
Admission: adult £2.40; child £1.20

Chedworth Roman Villa

In an area full of fine churches, the 12th-century **St John's** at Elkstone (off A417 south of Crickley Hill) probably takes the prize for having the most complicated decor on the simplest structure. Outside, look at the carved tympanum and the beak head decoration of the arch around it. A figure lies upside down grasping the snouts of creatures to either side. The interior is a single space with no aisle. See the carving on the chancel arch, the intricately carved Jacobean pulpit and the spiral staircase behind it leading to a dovecote.

The **Green Dragon Inn** lies in a wooded coombe near the River Churn at Cockleford, half a mile north from Elkstone. It's a country pub with a couple of bars and three large eating areas. The ceilings are low, the walls and floors are bare stone, cool in the summer and cheery in the winter with huge log fires. The food, mostly salad, quiche and steak, is well cooked and served in generous portions. The ploughman's lunch comes with thick slices of home cured ham, pickles and salad. Real ales include Hook Norton, Old Peculier and Wadworths 6X. Last orders: lunch 2pm; dinner 10pm.

☆ CRICKLEY HILL COUNTRY PARK

On a high point of the Cotswold scarp to the east of Gloucester, this well-organised country park has something for everyone. Start with a picnic (tables and barbecue areas provided) while you contemplate the possibilities. There are self-guided walking trails over 150 acres designed for the archaeologist, the natural historian, the geologist, the botanist, plus a gentle stroll for families with young children. The Visitor Centre, the information boards and the wardens are all helpful.

View from Crickley Hill

The highest point is a neolithic site: people looked out over this same vale below 5,500 years ago. Successive settlement areas have been marked out, and because the ground is oolitic limestone (the stuff of dry stone walls), which has never been ploughed, much of the archaeological evidence lies just beneath the surface. There are digs here every summer.

There are natural beech and oak woods, scrub and grassland and, since the area has never been treated with chemicals, the plant life is marvellously varied. The yellow and white Eyebright is a Crickley Hill speciality. Bring your plant identification book.

✪ GLOUCESTER

The Tailor of Gloucester with his cat Simpkin and Dr Foster who went to Gloucester are symbols of a city that is as familiar in rhyme and legend as it is important in English history. The Romans were in Gloucester and it was from here that William the Conqueror issued instructions for the great inventory we call the Domesday Book. Gloucester Cathedral witnessed the coronation and burial of English monarchs, and Gloucester's inland dock was an important waterway for trade.

More's the pity, then, that the modern city centre, with the exception of the dockside, is such a mess of poor planning and worse development. The docks are certainly worth seeing though, and the cathedral alone would be sufficient reason to visit Gloucester. The **Tourist Information Centre** is in Southgate Street; tel. 0452 421188.

The layout of the city is simple, based on the Roman principle of constructing gates at the four points of the compass from the centre. **Gloucester Cathedral** lies between Northgate Street and Westgate Street. Though originally Norman, most of it is built in the Perpendicular style. The vast Norman pillars of the nave, the 14th-century east window commemorating the battle of Crécy, the sumptuous fan vaulting of the cloisters (the earliest of its kind in England) and the beautiful Lady Chapel more than make up for the unbeautiful modern city.

Look for the elaborate alabaster tomb of Edward II, murdered at Warwick Castle in 1327. Pilgrims flocking to his shrine made Gloucester a wealthy city. Nearby, the less exalted tomb of

Thomas Machin and his wife, married for 50 years, shows their seven sons and six daughters kneeling in prayer at the base, the littlest ones squeezed round the sides like sardines.

The very pleasant **Undercroft Restaurant** next to the cathedral shop beneath the cloisters is open from 10am-5pm. Lunch is served from noon-2.30pm. The food is genuinely home-made and delicious.

Leaving the cathedral by College Court, you'll find the **Beatrix Potter Shop and Museum** also has its pilgrims. This tiny house was chosen by Beatrix Potter to be the model for the tailor's house in *The Tailor of Gloucester*. The story had some basis in fact. A tailor did indeed leave an unfinished waistcoat overnight in his shop and on his return next morning found the work mysteriously completed, bar one buttonhole. He claimed the work had been done by fairies. Beatrix Potter reworked it with animal characters. The original tailor's house is now part of the timber-framed pub in Westgate Street, The Tailor's House.

The shop is bursting with soft toys, plates, mugs and other Beatrix Potter merchandise. There are also early editions of her books, drawings, and letters which reveal a keen business acumen. The superb embroidered waistcoat with a note attached, 'No more twist', was not made by mice or fairies but by members of the local Women's Institute.

As you emerge from College Court, turn right down Westgate Street to the timber-framed Tudor building which houses the **Gloucester Folk Museum**. This is a most cheerful and interesting place to learn how Gloucester people have lived and worked through the ages. The first floor was the premises of a pin factory from mid 18th-19th century so there's a real feel of authenticity about the museum. Huge basket-work salmon and eel traps indicate Gloucester's former reliance on river fishing. School children are invited to put on Victorian schoolclothes and cheerfully attend the Victorian classroom, to be taught an old-fashioned lesson. (Small parties should ask to have a go, too.) Younger ones love the stuffed cow and Gloucester Old Spot pig.

Opening times: daily Jul-Sept; Mon-Sat the rest of the year
Admission: free

Gloucester's 19th-century Docks, now a hive of leisure activity

Continue down Westgate Street and follow the signs left for Maritime Walk. Cross a busy road and you are in **Gloucester Docks**, a genuine set of 19th-century docks now converted into an appealing entertainment and leisure centre, including some of Gloucester's best museums. To your right, as you enter, is the **Gloucester Antiques Centre**. This old warehouse, said to attract more tourists than the cathedral itself, is open every day of the week. Antique furniture is found on the ground floor, and the rest of the building is leased to around 60 dealers selling lace, jewellery, prints, china and so on. Some of it is tat and some not. The small café on one of the upper floors - The Place on the Lock - has great views of the dock and the vessels moored there.

The modern glass and steel building on the main dock basin is Merchants Quay, a smart riverside complex of shops and restaurants. Everybody makes for **Dr Fosters** pub and restaurant, full of warehouse memorabilia, which is long on atmosphere, but short on speedy service. If you are in no hurry, it's an enjoyable place to linger. Last orders for restaurant and bar meals are: lunch 2pm; dinner 10pm.

The **Robert Opie Collection** in Albert Warehouse, otherwise the Museum of Advertising and Packaging, is an intriguing collection of the sort of things that people have been chucking into their dustbins since the 1880s. Old tins and jars and wrappers chart our social history by indicating what we consume and how we are persuaded to do so. The naïveté of early television commercials shown here provokes unbelieving mirth in young viewers. There is a tea room and gift and book shop.

Robert Opie Collection, Albert Warehouse. Tel: 0452 302309
Opening times: Tues-Sun 10am-6pm; closed Christmas and Boxing Day
Admission: adult £2.25; child 85p

It's just a short step onwards to the **National Waterways Museum** in Llanthony Warehouse. If you've been confused by how Gloucester, an inland city, has docks, dredgers and sailing ships, all will be revealed here. The history of Gloucester's canals and waterways, how and why they were built and the daily life of the people who worked in them, is well documented in

archive film, sound recordings and working models. It is a pow-
erfully evocative and unsentimental exhibition. Outside the
museum, blacksmiths and carpenters demonstrate their work for
summer visitors. Guided walking tours of the docks leave from
the National Waterways Museum on Sundays at 2.30pm and last
an hour - extremely good if you want a wider frame of reference
for your visit.

National Waterways Museum, Llanthony Warehouse. Tel: 0452 307009
Opening times: daily 10am-5pm (6pm in summer); closed Christmas Day
Admission: adult £3.25; child £2.25

The last museum of note on Gloucester Docks is the **Regiments
of Gloucestershire Military Museum** in the old Custom House
behind Victoria Dock. The emphasis here is on presenting the
human and social aspects of soldiering rather than a mass of old
weapons and uniforms - although they're here too. Unusual
among military museums, this one covers the lives of soldiers'
wives or widows and brings the history of the regiments to the
present day. A flak jacket worn by an officer serving in Northern
Ireland who survived a round of bullets fired at close range from
a submachine gun leaves one's jaws agape.

Regiments of Gloucestershire Military Museum, Commercial Road. Tel: 0452 522682
Opening times: Tues-Sun & Bank Hol Mons 10am-5pm
Admission: adult £2.50; child £1.25

Queen Boadicea II, a veteran of the Dunkirk landings, leaves
from Merchants Quay for a gentle 40-minute trip down the
Gloucester and Sharpness Canal. As you pass the dry dock
where boats are being refitted, you may catch a glimpse of the
square-rigged sailing ships used in television series like *The
Onedin Line*, filmed here in Gloucester. The canal-side is being
tidied up and old warehouses are pulled down to reveal older
buildings like 12th-century Llanthony Priory, hitherto hidden
from the water. The landscape becomes progressively greener,
though, to be honest, despite occasional sightings of kingfishers
and cormorants, it is never pastoral. As the boat nears
Hempsted Bridge, the road traffic is stopped and a man winds
the bridge open to allow the boat through. At Two Mile Bend, it
turns for the return journey. Queen Boadicea II operates three
trips a day from Easter-October departing at noon, 2.30 and
3.30pm. Adult £1.75; child £1.25. For more information, telephone the National Waterways Museum: 0452 307009.

⭐ **PAINSWICK**

Painswick stands on a steep spur of land between two valleys on the western edge of the Cotswold escarpment. A compact, elegant town, hardly more than a village, it boasts over 100 listed buildings, a famous church and churchyard, a good hotel, friendly pubs and opportunities for walking on nearby Painswick Beacon and in the ancient beech woods of Cranham.

The A46 bisects the town and in the summer, particularly in August, when the Gloucester Guild of Craftsmen sets up its stalls, Painswick can be as busy as any Cotswold tourist honeypot. The town falls steeply down the valley on one side of the road to Painswick Brook at the bottom. The stream, now a trickle, used to power the nine cloth mills that provided employment for the weavers and profits for the merchants in the 17th and 18th centuries. Some of the old mills are now holiday apartments.

Painswick's 11th-century church, restored in the 15th, still bears the scars of the Civil War. The grand Renaissance table tombs of cloth merchants and their families show carved decoration at its most sumptuous. You can pick up a tomb trail from the church. Then there is the matter of the magical yew trees. Some say there are 99 of them in the churchyard and the 100th can never grow. Others claim that it is impossible to count the trees and arrive at a number that agrees with anyone else - it's never been done. But it's a good way of keeping the children busy while you look around the town.

The famous 'Clipping' ceremony takes place each year on the Sunday following September 19. It derives from an old English word, 'clyppan', meaning 'to embrace'. Children from Painswick and surrounding parishes come together to hold hands round the church and embrace it. Boys wearing buttonholes and girls in garlands sing to the music of a band while the adults watch from among the yews and tombs. The words reveal the ceremony as a Victorian revival of a much earlier rite and the chorus goes:

'Oh that I had wings of angels
Here to spread and wings to fly
I would seek the gates of Zion
Far beyond the starry sky'.

The children then get a sugar bun - supplied by Painswick Bakery - and 10p each.

From local customs to local handicrafts, the **Painswick Antiques and Craft Centre** has premises on two floors of a converted Georgian chapel in New Street. You'll find antique furniture downstairs. Upstairs, the range of crafts displayed includes dried flowers from Buckley, children's clothes from Sheepscombe, pretty patchwork quilts from Painswick. Open every day. For high-quality work in wood, see Dennis French's shop, recently opened in New Street, called Woodcraft. You will find other examples of his work in the Visitor Centre at Westonbirt Arboretum (see Day 6).

The **Dream Factory** in Friday Street is where Jo Palmer, a modern tailor of Painswick, works in two tiny rooms on the ground floor. She sews in one room and does her fittings in the other. Trained by Worth, she specializes in ballgowns and wedding dresses - the stuff of dreams, indeed - though she will run up simpler numbers for you. Her clients include the rich and famous - of whom there are many in Gloucestershire.

Painswick Rococo Garden, half a mile north of the town, belongs to Lord Dickinson of Painswick House who is in the process of restoring it from wild woodland to the original rococo style (formal but not geometric) designed by his forebears in the 1740s. The work is far from complete but there are walks and vistas and hidden pavilions in these six-and-a-half acres and a lively feeling of work in progress. Whether it is worth the entrance fee to walk around an unfinished 18th-century garden while you are in the midst of so much free natural beauty depends on your own personal preference.

There is, though, a very good licensed restaurant in the grounds serving home-made food, and Painswick House is open to visitors most Sundays during the summer. If you are here in February and March, be sure to see the display of the special variety of large snowdrop called 'galanthus atkinsii', after a Painswick nurseryman called Atkins.

Painswick Rococo Garden, Painswick - access from B4073. Tel: 0452 813208
Opening times: Feb 1 - mid-Dec Wednes-Sun 11am-5pm
Admission: adult £2.40; child £1.20

A Painswick Mansion

☆ PRINKNASH ABBEY

Unusually for the Cotswolds, this thoroughly modern monastic community has nothing to do with wool but makes a living out of pottery. Prinknash (pronounced 'Prinnage') Abbey, on the green and rolling lower slopes of the escarpment between Birdlip and Painswick, is a Benedictine foundation which opened here in 1972. The abbey (on your right as you enter the car park) is built in Cotswold Guiting stone but looks like a pink 1950s office block.

The Abbey Church is a small private chapel for the monks but open to the public. (There is Low Mass at 7am, Sung Mass at 11.30am and Vespers at 6pm.) The ironwork, carpentry, the stained glass and the organ were all made by members of the community.

> The old Abbey, **St Peter's Grange**, was formerly a hunting lodge for the abbots of Gloucester. It is just a short stroll from the new abbey along a tarred road through parkland. Follow the arrows from the car park towards the abbey which stands on what Horace Walpole, writing in 1774, described as a 'glorious but impracticable hill, in the midst of a little forest of beech and commanding Elysium'.

Prinknash Abbey: St Peter's Grange and stained glass window in the Abbey Church

It was only when the foundations for the new abbey were being dug that the clay which finances this community was discovered. Now the pottery, run by the monks but mostly staffed by local potters, is a commercial concern. You can see the work in progress through a large window, and if you time your visit while there is a commentary from a guide so much the better, but it's not essential.

The monks still produce their own particular style of pottery - a black lustre pewter-glazed ware - dramatic or flashy, according to taste. They also make incense and rosaries, widely sold abroad and in the shop that sells only Prinknash products. There is another shop for general gifts and a self-service snack bar, where you can buy herbs and jams and chutneys made by the monks. You are left with a feeling the monks of this abbey have lost none of the commercial expertise of their wool-gathering predecessors.

Prinknash Pottery, Prinknash Abbey, Cranham - access from A46. Tel: 0452 812239
Opening times: Mon-Sat 10.30am-4pm & Sun pm
Admission: adult 75p; child 45p

On a more spiritual note, Prinknash Abbey welcomes visitors to chapel services and offers simple accommodation for those who want a contemplative holiday or retreat.

Prinknash Bird Park, a short walk down the hill from the pottery, is a private venture, independent of the abbey. In nine acres, it has a variety of waterfowl, pheasants, peacocks, a deer park and a trout pond with fish so big and greedy they look as though they'd jump out to take a bite out of your hand. There is one small aviary for budgerigars but no other birds are caged. Again the question arises: do you want to pay to see a man-made natural environment when you are already surrounded by the real thing?

Prinknash Bird Park, Prinknash Abbey, nr Cranham - access from A46.
Tel: 0452 812727
Opening times: daily Apr-Oct 10am-5pm
Admission: adult £2.50; child £1.30

> If you can squeeze them in, pass through the tiny hamlets along the River Dunt (little more than a stream) on the western side of A417: Daglingworth (Saxon carvings in church, part of the Duchy of Cornwall), Duntisbourne Rouse (minuscule church clinging to a hill, with mediaeval wall paintings), Middle Duntisbourne (mind the ducks in the ford), Duntisbourne Leer, so called because it once belonged to the Abbey of Lire in Normandy (houses round a ford), and Duntisbourne Abbots, so named because it once belonged to the abbots of Gloucester (most substantial of the villages, with a Norman church). All are delightful places.

☆ SLAD

The poet Laurie Lee spent the early years of his life in this village and wrote about it in his autobiographical novel *Cider With Rosie*. You would have to get out of the car and spend time walking deep in the woods to recapture, however faintly, the spirit of his Gloucestershire childhood in the 1920s. The village is cut in half by the busy Birdlip-Stroud road but the Lee house is still there, and the Woolpack Inn, a real country pub. The Star pub and the Old School House are now private houses. The squire's house,

Steenbridge, a Tudor house with a Georgian façade, is also still there, as is the church and the chapel, and the pool where poor Miss Flynn drowned herself. The poet still takes an active interest in local affairs - most notably in joining the battle to keep the Butcher's Arms pub open in neighbouring Sheepscombe when the brewers were threatening to close it.

The Butcher's Arms, Sheepscombe

WHERE TO STAY

Painswick

🦮 🖐 🐴 🍽 £

Damsels Farm, *Painswick,*
Glos GL6 6UD
Tel: 0452 812148
Closed Dec

This is a small working sheep farm deep in a lovely wooded valley between Painswick and Sheepscombe. Before you reach Damsels Farm, you have to negotiate a couple of gates and drive along an untarred farm track. This is not a guesthouse for people who hate mud. There are three double rooms, furnished in an old-fashioned homely style. One has a shower and the other two share a bathroom. Charles II came down from reviewing his troops before the battle of Gloucester and called this area 'paradise'. Damsel's farm is on the 's' of the word 'paradise' on the OS map.

Painswick

🏠 ✕ 🖐 🐴 ▭ ££££

The Painswick Hotel, *Kemps Lane,*
Painswick, Glos GL6 6YB
Tel: 0452 812160
Open all year

This former rectory built in 1790 in Palladian style is undoubtedly the smartest hotel in Painswick, recently done up in the style of an elegant, private house, with strong colours and bold designs. The furniture is mostly antique and the owners have not stinted with the small decorative touches like a vase or a carving which give each room its own individual character. Many of the bedrooms have wonderful views of the Severn Valley. Guests are welcomed with a bowl of fruit, and even a game of Scrabble is provided in the bedroom. The public rooms are delightful with panelled walls, fine furniture, paintings and open fireplaces. The first-floor Regency drawing room, with window seats overlooking the valley, is a great success. The restaurant specialises in salmon and game and fresh shellfish from a seawater tank. Vegetables come from the Vale of Evesham. Wines are varied and well chosen, the dining room is elegant and restful. Last orders: lunch 2pm; dinner 9.30pm.

Slad

🦮 🖐10 🐴 🍽 ££

Down Court, *Slad, Glos GL6 7QE*
Tel: 0452 812427
Open all year

The interiors for the film of Laurie Lee's book *Cider with Rosie* were shot here at Down Court. The house was originally a row of 17th-century farm workers' cottages, now knocked together into a single dwelling. The two guest bedrooms, despite low ceilings and exposed beams, are light and airy, attractively decorated in country style, and furnished with some good antique furniture. The bathroom, though, is shared. A small sitting room downstairs and a large drawing room complete with grand piano are both available for use of guests. The owner, Anne Mills, is a trained chef and provides an excellent four-course evening meal for under £15.

Upton St Leonards
🏠 ✕ 🧍 🐴 �̶ ££££

Bowden Hall Resort Hotel, *Bondend
Lane, Upton St Leonards nr Gloucester,
Glos GL4 8ED*
Tel: 0452 614121
Open all year
This Grade II listed building in extensive grounds has recently been completely refurbished. It has 72 bedrooms, a leisure and health club and
conference facilities and caters for the
business executive, but also does a
good trade in weekend packages for
families. The parkland and lake are
beautiful for those who want only a
gentle potter outdoors between read-
ing in the lounge and drinking in the
bar. The energetic are well catered
for with a pool, sauna and gym.
Considering Gloucester's lack of
good class accommodation, it also
makes a useful base for sightseeing.
Decoration is mostly floral without
being twee or fussy. The perks of an
executive room include a decanter of
sherry or spirits and your own
bathrobe. The views from many of
the rooms are lovely. Last orders in
the hotel restaurant, **Dearman's**, are:
lunch 1.30pm; dinner 9pm.

Upton St Leonards
🏠 ✕ 🧍 🚌 ££££

Hatton Court Hotel, *Upton Hill,
Upton St. Leonards nr. Gloucester,
Glos GL4 8DE*
Tel: 0452 617412
Open all year
Situated 600 feet up on the edge of
the Cotswold escarpment, this hotel
commands sweeping views of the
Malvern Hills and the Severn Valley,
as well as its own extensive grounds.
The hotel capitalises on the view, but
everything else is pretty luxurious
too. The original structure of the
house is 17th century but it has been
extended and improved. Out of 46
rooms, all individually decorated, all
of them spacious, 15 are classed as
superior - with the full range of services including Jacuzzis, fruit, biscuits, tea- and coffee-making facilities
and free in-house movies, bathrobes
and a cuddly teddy bear. Guests may
also use the decent-sized heated outdoor swimming pool open from May
to October. The restaurant,
Carrington's, offers a sensible
'starters and pudding' menu. Last
orders: lunch 2pm; dinner 10pm.

WHERE TO EAT

Birdlip
✕ 🚌 £££

Kingshead House, *Birdlip*
Tel: 0452 862299
Lunch Tues-Fri & Sun; dinner Tues-Sat
This 17th-century former coaching
inn is now a first class restaurant run
by Judy and Warren Knock. Judy is
not keen on categorising her own
cooking but, when pressed, describes
it as 'mostly British'. Three courses
might include pheasant and wild
mushroom soup, roast fillet of local

beef with mustard and horseradish
sauce and an iced pudding from an
1860 recipe. Beside the restaurant
(exposed stone wall, low beamed
ceilings and polished wooden floor)
there is also a small bar and cosy
lounge. Live classical guitar music
livens up the first Friday of the
month. Last orders: lunch 2pm; dinner 10pm. There is also bed and
breakfast accommodation in a double bedroom, own bathroom, on the
first floor.

Cranham
📦 ✉ ££

The Black Horse, *Cranham, nr*
Painswick
Tel: 0452 812217
Open all year: bar meals daily; R dinner
Fri & Sat only
'We haven't cooked a chip in six
years,' says the chef/landlady of this
pub and restaurant. The emphasis is
on fresh, home-made food, both in
the bar and in the first-floor restaurant. The landlord is a former game-
keeper and justly proud of his seasonal game dishes. The Black Horse
has been a pub for the last 200 years.
It's off the beaten track in a delightful
valley overlooking the beechwoods
of Cranham, and a jealously guarded
secret for those in the know. It's old-
fashioned with wood-panelled walls
and quarry stone floor. Last orders:
bar - lunch 2pm; dinner 9pm. It is
advisable to book for the restaurant.

Painswick
📦 ✉ ££

Royal Oak, *St. Mary's Street,*
Painswick
Tel: 0452 813129
Open all year
Bang in the centre of the village, this
pub is popular with locals as well as
visitors. A huge open fire divides the
room into two bar areas and there is
a small conservatory facing a floral
courtyard. The whole place is small,
cosy and welcoming. Good-value bar
meals range from home-made pâté to
steak and kidney pie or roast pork
and two veg. This is a real ale pub
serving Boddingtons, Flowers
Original and Whitbreads PA.

Slad
✖ ▭ ££££

Oakes, *169 Slad Road, Stroud*
Tel: 0453 759950
Closed 2 wks Aug and a mth over
Christmas; closed Sun eve and Mon
You could easily drive past and miss
this modest looking 19th-century former girls' school, now a restaurant
run by Chris and Caroline Oakes.
Once inside, the emphasis is on good
food imaginatively prepared and a
relaxed atmosphere rather than fussy
decor and a fancy menu. The restaurant is a single room, with plain polished wooden floor covered by rugs,
plain white linen on the tables and
only flowers and candles for decoration. Chris Oakes believes in using
the best produce and lists the names
of local suppliers at the front of his
menu. It's advisable to book. Last
orders: lunch 1.45pm; dinner 9.30pm.

CIRENCESTER AND THE EASTERN WOLDS

From the harmonious contours of hill and vale the eastern wolds slide gently down into the lush flatness of the upper Thames Valley. Here the waters of the Churn, the Coln and the Leach become the River Thames. Cirencester is the eastern capital of the Cotswolds and not to be missed for its top class museum, its parish church, and, above all, for its general good cheer. Gardeners can visit Rosemary Verey's famous garden at Barnsley for ideas and cuttings. If the weather looks murky, the Cotswold Woollen Weavers are under cover and it's always a pleasure to watch someone else working.

Near Lechlade, Kelmscott House, home of William Morris, is open only on Wednesday, so that's one easy choice. Was Morris right in thinking Bibury the most beautiful village in England? Or would any of the quieter settlements along the Coln have a better claim to the title? Judge for yourself. And if you wished, you could spend a day on the beach. The Cotswold Water Park, with its hundred-odd gravel lakes fed by underground springs, offers a range of water sports as well as gentler pleasures like birdwatching.

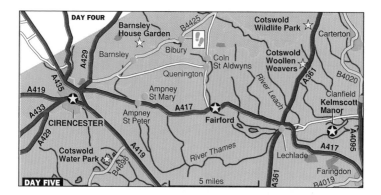

☆ BARNSLEY HOUSE GARDEN

This private garden attached to a late 17th-century house is essentially the lifetime creation of one woman, Rosemary Verey. Encouraged by her late husband, David, an eminent architectural historian of the county, she first opened the garden to the public 30 years ago.

It is organised quite informally. If you don't know your plants, there's no choice but to wander and admire, because no explanatory material or labelling is provided. Apart from the flowers, special features include the herb garden, the knot garden, adapted from three to four hundred year old gardening patterns, and the potager, or vegetable garden. This is a formally planted area, separated by paths and small box hedges, with peas and beans, lettuces and cabbages, lavender, thyme, roses, all placed with as much care for design, shape and colour as any conventional flower garden. Just don't try picking a lettuce for your lunch, that's all.

There are plants and cuttings for sale. The speciality of the house is a mallow – *lavatera Barnsley* – a white flower with a delicate pink centre. There's also a room full of small country antiques as well as modern furniture - a business enterprise of the younger Vereys. The house is not open to the public.

Leave the car park and turn right for the 12th-century church of St Mary. Opposite is The Village Pub, whose dramatically paint-

Barnsley House Garden

The Village Pub's award-winning sign, Barnsley

ed sign has been the subject of some critical interest. Not just the sign, but the food and the beer win local commendations. Look around you. No telegraph wires, no poles. One of the advantages of being an estate village is that someone has paid for all these useful but unsightly appurtenances of modern life to be buried or hidden away.

Barnsley House Garden, Barnsley. Tel: 0285 740281
Opening times: Mon, Wednes, Thurs, Sat 10am-6pm
Admission: adult £2, children free

'*Come down, O, love divine...*' are the opening words of the composer Ralph Vaughan Williams's most famous hymn. He called the tune 'Down Ampney' after his birthplace, five miles southeast of Cirencester and one of a group of **'Ampney'** villages. The rectory at Down Ampney where he was born in 1872 and lived his early life stands at one end of the village, visible from the road but not open to the public. His father Arthur Vaughan Williams was vicar at the church of All Saints (originally 13th-century but heavily restored in the 19th) which has a window commemorating his life.

BIBURY WALK

An hour-long circular walk takes you past all the principle sights in Bibury. Begin at the excellent pub, the Catherine Wheel, to the south-west of the village. (Open from 11am - 11pm. Fresh trout a speciality. Special children's menu.) Take the footpath beside the car park, passing along the left-hand side of a field and over a stile. There are different signposted footpaths at this stage. To keep the walk within the hour, choose the sign that points straight ahead. Walk towards some tall beeches, past the cricket pitch, fenced to keep out stock, leaving the pavilion on your right. There are views of Bibury's cream and grey roofs though the beech trees to your left.

As you pass through gates at the end of the field, a wider landscape of fields and woods and a silver arc of river open out before you. Come down the track, turn left at the bottom and follow the bridleway. Prosperous houses cluster round the rushing confluence of mill race and river. The only tatty building is the old mill. If you peer in through the windows, you'll see the mill wheel still clanking round. On your left are the lawns of Bibury Court Hotel.

Walk to the tarred road and turn left towards the village. The second turn to your left brings you down to the church (Anglo-Saxon origins) and a sweet little square surrounded by 17th- and 18th-century cottages. Back on the B4225, cross the bridge to The Rack Island, the water meadow where in the heyday of the weaving industry cloth was laid to dry on racks, now a National Trust wildfowl reserve. You are now officially in a separate hamlet called Arlington really a continuation of Bibury. To your left are the famous **Arlington Mill Weavers' Cottages**, a long terrace of lichen-speckled houses with higgledy-piggledy gables and doors: quite a sight, though none of them is open to the public. The River Coln runs shallow and clear beside them.

Follow the river round The Rack Island and cross the road to the old mill, now the **Arlington Mill Museum**, straight ahead of you. Its 17 exhibition rooms include old-fashioned blacksmith's and wheelwright's shops, a William Morris-style room and pieces of furniture made by members of the Cotswold Arts and Crafts Movement, none of it that compelling or well displayed. The best exhibit is the working mill dating from the 18th century, though not originally from this site.

Arlington Mill Museum, Bibury. Tel: 0285 74368
Opening times: daily mid-Mar - mid-Nov; weekends only in winter; 10.30am-7pm or dusk if earlier
Admission: adult £2, child £1 →

Just beyond the mill is **Bibury Trout Farm**, established in 1902. Whatever your feelings about the ecological rights and wrongs of trout farms, this one is at least diverting. Among its 14 acres of ponds separated by pleasant grassy walkways, lively with ducks and moorhens, the fish are reared for sale. They (and their eggs) mostly go to re-stock other farms and reservoirs, often abroad.

The farm is well organised for visitors. You can sit in the sun beside the ponds watching the fish leap for the food you toss to them (20p a cup) and if you want to do some fishing, it's £1 for the rod and £1.80 for every pound you catch. There is a general gift shop as well as a delicatessen, plus the opportunity to buy fresh and smoked trout and plants too, as you leave. Asian Britons, anxious for undisputably fresh fish, are apparently among the keenest customers.

Bibury Trout Farm, Bibury. Tel: 0285 74215
Opening times: daily except Christmas Day and Boxing Day, 9am-5pm in winter, 9am-6pm in summer; Sun 10am-6pm
Admission: adult £1.80, child 90p

From the farm, make your way up the hill back to your starting point, the Catherine Wheel, to end the walk.

Old houses beside the calm, trout-filled waters of the river Coln make **Quenington** one of the loveliest villages in the eastern wolds. Bridge, rectory, mill and 600-year-old Quenington Court, a manor house which once belonged to the Knights Hospitallers, complete the picture. But the star of Quenington is undoubtedly the **Church of St Oswald**, which stands at one end of the village and is worth visiting for at least three reasons. Firstly, for its setting at the turn of the river; secondly, for its two extraordinary carved porches; and thirdly, for the embroidered blue kneelers depicting all the ordinary flowers, birds and beasts of the countryside such as newts, rabbits, and a mouse eating a blade of grass.

✪ CIRENCESTER

This is a lively town, a satisfying mix of old and new. Enough of the old Roman walls still stand to remind you that as Corinium, Cirencester was, for about 350 years, the second largest Roman city in England. Modern day 'Ciren' is a busy market town - frequented these days more by agricultural students than by farmers - with an excellent reputation for crafts, a magnificent parish church and more green space within its centre than many a leafy suburb.

The centre of Cirencester is dominated by its Market Place and the 15th-century parish church of **St John the Baptist** at one end of it. With its soaring tower and Perpendicular three-storeyed south porch, as high as the church itself, the whole is a glorious testimony to the wealth created by wool. Of the treasures inside the most famous is the Boleyn Cup, made for Queen Anne Boleyn in 1535, a rare survival of Tudor silver and kept safely in a glass case. Take time to wander in the grounds of the old abbey behind the church (of which nothing remains bar the Norman gatehouse at Spital Gate). The grounds form a substantial part of the town's green area and - with part of the Roman wall still standing and the River Churn teeming with waterfowl - make a good place to stretch your legs, perhaps have a picnic.

Cirencester: The Parish Church of St John the Baptist on the High Street and The Bear Inn

If you'd rather sit down and be served lunch, you are already very close to **Harry Hare's Brasserie and Restaurant** in Gosditch Street, opposite the church. It is one large room - plain wooden floorboards, bentwood chairs and wooden tables - leading out to a patio and a pleasant walled garden. Hare's home-made fish cakes are the speciality of the house. Open 11am-11pm every day.

The town's history reveals itself readily through its streets. For the sights of 17th- and 18th-century Cirencester, the triangle formed by Coxwell, Dollar and Thomas Streets is the most productive; for the Roman town, the grassed mound of the amphitheatre is a short walk to the south of town.

In the centre itself, the **Corinium Museum**, recently reorganised and extended, is the most entertaining and instructive guide to Cirencester's history, particularly its Roman period. Large mosaics, found locally, of which the most famous are the Hunting Dogs and Four Seasons, and the Jupiter column with huge Corinthian capital, are the star exhibits. The museum is open throughout the year except winter Mondays, and at £1 for adults, 50p for children, well worth a visit.

If you climbed the church tower (only possible now with permission of the vicar) you would see the grounds of **Cirencester Park**, virtually a stone's throw away, surrounded by a vast yew hedge. The house, home of the Bathurst family, built early in the 18th century, is closed to the public, but the park is open from 8am-5pm. Alexander Pope, the poet, joined his great friend, the 1st Earl Bathurst, 'to draw plans for houses and gardens, open avenues... all very fine and beautiful in our own imagination'. They were equally fine in reality as you will discover. Enter the park from Cecily Hill and immediately you are in Broad Avenue, a noble tree-lined avenue which runs for about four miles westwards to the village of Sapperton. On summer Sundays polo matches are played in the park, scene of the Royal arm breakage.

Don't leave town without visiting the **Cirencester Workshops** on Cricklade Street. This former brewery is now occupied on three floors by a busy hive of sculptors, jewellers, textile designers, bookbinders, weavers etc. Wander round, stop for a chat. There's a comradely air about the place, with radios playing and people shouting their sandwich orders across to each other. The Coffee House on the first floor serves teas and coffees, milkshakes and home-made cakes. Try the delicious apple and cinammon baked cheesecake. The workshops are open Monday-Saturday, 10am-5pm.

Few would deny that Cirencester is poor in fine restaurants but rich in **good foodshops**. There is an excellent food market on Friday. At Number One, at the end of Market Place, Windrush Wines are true pioneers in seeking out interesting, different, rather esoteric wines. Prices represent amazingly good value. Pop into Barnett on the corner for famously fresh fish. Turn right, then left into Blackjack Street and at no. 14, Jesse Smith is chief among butchers. The speciality is Aberdeen Angus beef, organic meat, wild boar and other game.

☆ COTSWOLD WATER PARK

Two areas of lake - former gravel extraction pits - form the basis of the Cotswold Water Park, for water sports and general leisure activities. You'll find the larger group of lakes to the south of Cirencester around Somerford Keynes (pronounced Keens) and the smaller, south of the A417 between Fairford and Lechlade. In total there are over 100 lakes, all numbered, offering a variety of activities ranging from swimming to jet ski-ing, sailing, surfing and coarse and game fishing. Some have restricted club member-ship, others are open to the public to hire equipment and use on a daily basis. The lakes are variously owned by private individu-als, consortia, or local authorities.

The easiest way to see what is on offer and decide what you want to do is to head for Keynes Country Park on Lakes 31,32 and 33, speak to the warden and pick up useful leaflets and information. It costs £3 to park your car here for a day. On these three closely adjoining lakes there is a small, sheltered beach for younger children and a larger family beach; there are also play and picnic areas. You can hire rowing boats and pedalos, and fish by the day or half-day. The park is rich in bird life and wild-fowl and use of bird hides is free. Seasonal walking routes lead you through the likeliest places to see particular birds, plants or insects.

Windsurfing in Cotswold Water Park

Some of the newer pits look a little raw and tatty at the edges but those longer established are often pleasantly wooded. Swimming is strictly forbidden outside designated areas because the sides of the lakes often shelve very steeply and the spring-fed water is particularly cold.

Cotswold Water Park, Keynes Country Park, Shorn Cote, Cirencester. Tel: 0285 861459
Spinerd Sailboards on Lake 10 hire out surfboards, canoes, dinghies and mountain bikes. Steel-Away (0285 851356) also hire bikes at £12.50 per day with a £50 cheque deposit

North Meadow, a 110-acre plot just outside Cricklade, must be one of the smallest nature reserves in the country. This ancient hay meadow has been preserved for hundreds of years by an ancient law which permits the people of the village grazing rights on the meadow from Lammas to Lady Day (August 12-February 12) and one cut of hay when the grass has grown back. Now the meadow is important for its rare plants and flowers. In early summer, for example, there are more snake's head fritillaries in a small corner of North Meadow than in the whole of the rest of the country. Not ostentatiously signposted, it lies north of Cricklade, on the left, just as you see a sign for Cotswold Water Park.

COTSWOLD WILDLIFE PARK

This is a 120-acre park set around a large manor house. If you are expecting a zoo, you may be disappointed. There are no elephants, lions or tigers. But there are leopards, camels, zebra, rhino, monkeys, small mammals, a reptile house, an aquarium, a tropical house and a butterfly house. The policy is to allow the animals as much freedom and space as possible and keep cages to the minimum. The rhino and zebra enclosure has a ha ha around it - a deep ditch walled on one side - a clever way of securing livestock without unsightly fencing. It dates from the days when this was a private estate whose owners wanted to enjoy an uninterrupted view of lawn and parkland. Some of the larger animals may be viewed only from a distance.

The grounds are well laid out and proper attention is paid to plants and flowers as well as animals. The walled garden proves a haven for many an exhausted grandparent. The tropical house, ablaze with bougainvillaea, hibiscus, and bird of paradise flower, has free-flying tropical birds swooping among the vegetation and giant coy carp floating lazily in the pool.

Penguins entertaining visitors to Cotswold Wildlife Park

Children's entertainments include a narrow gauge railway that runs around the park in summer months, an adventure playground and animal brass rubbings in the manor itself. Young visitors prove keen adoptive parents of the park animals, even the griffon vultures. Wheelchairs are free and readily available.

Cotswold Wildlife Park, Burford - access from A361. Tel: 0993 823006
Opening times: daily, except Christmas Day, 10am-6pm or dusk
Admission: adult £3.80, child £2.20

☆ COTSWOLD WOOLLEN WEAVERS

This is the only place in the Cotswolds where Cotswold wool is still woven. Here, in a converted stone barn in the village of Filkins, Jane and Peter Martin have been running a rural woollen mill, using traditional power looms (the oldest from 1862 but most from the turn of the century), since 1982. It's useful to pick up a free explanatory leaflet before you go in to watch the (mostly young) people operating the looms. There's a fearful clacking while the machinery is working - the weavers wear headphones - and a pervasive smell of car mechanics' jerseys, a heady mix of wool and oil.

Upstairs there are more looms and an exhibition of handlooms and artefacts connected with the history of wool in the Cotswolds. The shop, in a separate building, sells wool, made-up garments, hats and gloves. There is always a limited run of any cloth, so there are no exact repeats. The Weavers also accept commissions - anything from 20 to 2,000 yards. Ask specifically if you want to see something made from the wool of the original breed, the Cotswold Lion sheep. This wool comes from the Rare Breeds Survival Trust at Cotswold Farm Park, near Guiting Power (see Day Three). The rest, though not Cotswold, is British.

There is a small tea shop plus a picnic area in an orchard (borrow a Filkins-made rug). Craft workshops in nearby buildings house a potter, cabinet maker, a stone mason, and cane and rush workers.

The Cotswold Woollen Weavers, Filkins - access off A361 between Burford and
Lechlade. Tel: 0367 86491
Open daily, 10am-6pm, Sun 2pm-6pm
Admission: free

✪ FAIRFORD

This is an ancient town on the banks of the River Coln, famous for its good fishing and its **Parish Church of St. Mary**. The church (another magnificent wool church), was the work of one family, wealthy cloth merchants from Cirencester. John Tame began rebuilding an earlier structure in the last years of the 15th century and his son Edmund went on to finish it as it stands now.

The complete set of 28 mediaeval windows in the church is famous. Rather like a doom painting, the series amounts to a lesson beginning with the Creation and ending with the Last Judgement. Each window, made by the craftsmen who were responsible for the windows of King's College Chapel, Cambridge, is numbered for easy identification. Some people find the amount of clear glass in the windows a disappointment, but others enjoy the resulting contrast with the deep blues, yellows and many shades of red and green. Window 15 is a particularly bloodcurdling lesson of virtue rewarded and vice getting its just desserts.

Mediaeval stained glass windows in Fairford's Parish Church of St Mary

The carved misericords in the chancel, rather harder to see, are another glory of the church, though purposefully everyday in tone. They depict scenes from ordinary life - reapers, geese, domestic violence: a wife pulls her husband by the hair, while labouring him with a paddle.

The market place and London Road, lined with late 17th- and 18th-century houses, are down the hill from the church. If you walk in the opposite direction and turn left, you will come to the river and an old mill, now a private dwelling, beside it. The view of the town from here is satisfyingly pastoral.

✪ KELMSCOTT MANOR

William Morris, artist, designer and craftsman, rented this house in the village of Kelmscott (pronounced Kemscot and variously spelt with one or two t's) from 1871 until he died in 1896. He is buried, with his family, in the churchyard.

It is a traditional stone house of the early 17th century with mullioned windows, gables and pediments and ball finials, and a graded pattern of lichen-covered roof slates which pleased Morris more than anything else. The house is full of his works, and those of his wife and friends, assembled here in the last 30 years. The house is therefore not as he left it, but it is not exactly a museum either. Every object is displayed with a care for its aesthetic effect that Morris would have applauded, and with enough natural light for things to be examined closely. The entry charge may seem high, but once inside, you'll agree it is worth it.

The rooms are hung with tapestry and pictures, patterns we are already familiar with from Sanderson fabrics like 'vine' and 'willow' and others that are a surprise. Embroidered wool hangings done by Morris himself are displayed alongside those designed by him but worked by his wife, Jane. There are drawings of her at various ages from 17 to 34 by their friend and co-habitant Dante Gabriel Rossetti, the tapestry room that was Rossetti's studio, carpets, chairs, the carved four-poster bed with bedspread embroidered by Jane. The valance was the work of their daughter, May, embroidered with a text written by her father, beginning:

'The wind's on the wold and the night is a-cold
And Thames runs chill twixt mead and hill

But kind and dear is the old house here
And my heart is warm midst winter's harm....'

Each item is labelled and the attendants are attentive and keen Morris fans so you don't need the accompanying booklet (£3), though it's nice to have. There is a refreshment and gift shop which also sells books. The house is run by the Society of Antiquaries.

The rest of this straggly village is quiet and rather subdued. Returning towards the centre you will come to the 'Memorial Cottages', on the left, erected by Jane after Morris's death. On the front façade there is a carving of Morris sitting cross-legged on the ground leaning against a tree. Further on, the Village Hall, designed by Ernest Gimson in memory of Morris, is looking the worse for wear. The Morris family gravestones are rather hidden by bushes in the graveyard of the parish church.

Kelmscott Manor, Kelmscott, nr Lechlade - access from A417. Tel: 0367 52486
Opening times: Apr-Sept 30, Wednes only, 11am-1pm & 2-5pm
Admission: adult £4, child £2

Fancy a game of *boules* beside the Thames? Not a very English sport perhaps, but **The Trout Inn** (on your left as you turn into the main Lechlade road from Kelmscot) has a *boules* pitch, as well as the traditional Oxfordshire game of Aunt Sally, in its riverside garden. It is also excellent for both food and liquid refreshment. Last orders: lunch 2pm; dinner 10pm.

WHERE TO STAY

Ampney St Mary

College Farm, *Ampney St Mary, nr Cirencester, Glos GL7 5SW*
Tel: 0285 851382
Open all year

College Farm is a working dairy farm in the centre of the tiny village of Ampney St Mary. The Bennetts offer a double bedroom, a twin-bedded room, and what might be described as a family suite: a double room right opposite a bunk-bedded room. All rooms have basins, tea- and coffee-making facilities, and are comfortably but not luxuriously furnished. The views are either of the back garden and the orchard or the front garden and the farm buildings. The bathroom is shared and there is a guest sitting room and dining room downstairs. A full English breakfast is served, as is a three-course evening meal, on request, for £7 per person. Vegetarians are also catered for.

Ampney St Peter
ᗺ ⫟10 ⨯ ££

Iveson House, *Ampney St. Peter,*
Cirencester, Glos GL7 5SH
Tel: 0285 851217
Open all year except over Christmas &
New Year
Susan and Peter Ansdell run their
attractive stone-built house in a way
which is a real advertisement for
Cotswold bed and breakfast accommodation. They offer their visitors a
double room or a twin-bedded room
with a private, though not connecting, bathroom to each. The garden is
a delightful three-acre spread, with
tennis court and swimming pool
(also for guest use). There is no
evening meal, but the Ansdells will
direct you to a nearby hostelry.

Bibury
⌂ ⨯ ⫟ ⇝ ▭ ££££

The Swan Hotel, *Bibury,*
Glos GL7 5NW
Tel: 0285 740 695
Open all year except 2 wks over
Christmas & New Year
This luxury hotel at one end of the
main bridge at Bibury is now under
new and private management. The
decor in the public rooms is in the
grand style - all chandeliers, deep red
carpet with repeating swan motif and
swagged curtains. All 18 bedrooms
are richly decorated and well
equipped, each with TV, telephone,
towelling robes - all the t's, in fact -
and a lot more besides. One of the 18
lacks a Jacuzzi bathroom but does
have a very efficient shower.
The Swan also runs a brasserie called
Jankowski's (the new owner is part
Polish and 'Jankowski' is Polish for
'swan') which is cheerful, spacious,
tolerant of walking shoes, and open
from 10am-10pm.

Clanfield
⌂ ⨯ ⫟ ▭ ££££

The Plough at Clanfield, *Bourton*
Road, Clanfield, Oxon OX8 2RB
Tel: 0367 81222
Open all year
The charm of this stone Elizabethan
house festooned in purple wisteria,
lies in its small size. It has only six
bedrooms. Each is palely luxurious,
restrained in decoration, but exceed-
ingly comfortable. Four have
whirlpool baths, the two attic rooms
have showers and share a bathroom
on the floor below. The Plough at
Clanfield is also known for its award-
winning restaurant. The Tapestry
Room (with tapestry hangings)
though small, is the main dining
room, beautifully decorated in soft
colours and fabrics. For a three-
course meal expect to pay just under
£30 per person. The service, as you
would expect, is good and attentive.

Coln St Aldwyns
⌂ ⨯ ⫟ ⇝ ▭ ££££

The New Inn, *Coln St Aldwyns,*
Cirencester, Glos GL7 5AN
Tel: 0285 750651
Open all year
Having escaped the threat of devel-
opers, the New Inn has re-opened
not just as a good local pub (which it
always was) but also as a restaurant
and extremely comfortable hotel.
Each bedroom, named after a neighbouring village, is individually decorated, those in the main house having
a slight edge in terms of luxury. All
have bathrooms, TV, telephone, etc.
The Dovecote annexe houses simpler
and cheaper rooms including a useful five-person family room.

WHERE TO EAT

Cirencester
📷 🚗 ££

The Oddfellows, *Chester Street, Cirencester*
Tel: 0285 641540
Open all year
This pub is tucked away in a residential street of terraced stone houses five minutes from the centre of Cirencester. It's basically one large room which leads into a conservatory, then a patio and garden. Familiar and friendly, it also has an enthusiastic local following.

Mary Stevens looks after the food while her husband, Francis, is in charge of drink, beer rather than lager and real ales the speciality. The decor is homely (apart from a new fruit machine) and the food is the best of home cooking. The blackboard menu is of the cottage pie, steak-and-kidney pudding variety. The more formal evening menu revolves around steak, fish and chicken. Last orders: lunch 2pm (Sun 12.30pm); dinner 9.30pm.

Cirencester
✕ 🚗 ££

Tatyan's, *27 Castle Street, Cirencester*
Tel: 0285 653529
Closed over Christmas; closed Sun lunch
This award-winning restaurant in the centre of Cirencester serves Cantonese, Szechuan, Hunan and Peking cuisine. Eschewing all pseudo-Chinese references in decor, Tatyan Cheung, publisher turned restaurateur, has kept his dining room light and simple - more Laura Ashley than Red Dragon. Crispy aromatic duck is a favourite but the steamed sea bass is much praised among British-Chinese patrons. Last orders: lunch 2pm; dinner 10.30pm. You'll find the cadet branch of Tatyan's at the Falcon Inn pub at Poulton just outside Cirencester. The food is slightly simpler and cheaper. Open pub hours.

Clanfield
📷 🚗 ££

The Clanfield Tavern, *Clanfield, Oxfordshire*
Tel: 0367 81223
Open all year
This cheerful, lively public house in the centre of Clanfield is as popular for its food as for its atmosphere. There are two chefs serving bar food as well as an *à la carte* restaurant. The bar menu ranges from snails in filo pastry to chicken livers with bacon and basil, salad and jacket potatoes for between £6 and £7. The restaurant menu is only slightly more formal, and helpings are generous. Everything is fresh and home made except the chips which are frozen. The real ales are all from Oxfordshire. Last orders: lunch 2pm; dinner 10pm.

The Clanfield Tavern also offers bed and breakfast. There are two double bedrooms with bathrooms, separate showers and bidets, £50 per room.

SOUTHWARDS
FROM STROUD

The hills and valleys of the wolds around Stroud begin to flat-
ten out by the time we reach the southern limits of this day's
tour. But the scarp remains steep on the western edge, providing
high look-out points over the Severn Vale. The landscape is an
abiding pleasure, particularly for walkers, who have the choice
of lofty, windswept commons, deep wooded coombes and footpaths beside canals, a reminder of the industrial history of the
southern wolds. Gliders and balloonists - on still days only - see
the same landscape from a different perspective. So do horse-
back riders, who can take advantage of bridleways through common lands. These scarcely exist in other parts of the Cotswolds.
Golfers have a choice of courses, mostly on the high plateau. If,
in all this idyllic countryside, you are looking for an officially
designated picnic spot, there's no better place than Westonbirt
Arboretum, unless it's Coaley Peak.

For a shot of culture, the lively Prema Arts Centre in Uley is
highly recommended. Slimbridge Wildfowl Centre, neighbouring Berkeley Castle and Jenner Museum, none of them strictly in
the Cotswolds but just over the border, are all worth the detour -
doubly so, if the weather turns against you. The hill-top towns of
Tetbury and Stroud show two different sides of the Cotswolds -
the former affluent and 'county', the latter less rarefied and full
of life.

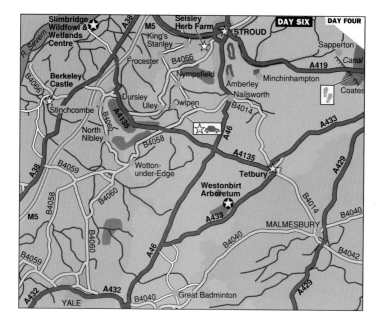

☆ BERKELEY CASTLE

This rather forbidding 12th-century fortress of red sandstone has for 24 generations been the home of the Berkeley family, whose hunting rights once stretched all the way from the Severn to London; both Berkeley Square in London and Berkeley University in California take their name from the family. In law, this estate can only pass to a male heir, while the title originally associated with it can pass through the direct female line. Thus ownership and title have been divided; the present incumbent is plain Mr Berkeley.

Paintings, tapestries, silver, china and furniture testify to the castle's longstanding domestic use. There's a lot to see, from the Great Hall, with its fine timber ceiling and minstrel's gallery, to the mediaeval kitchens, in use until the 1940s. The castle also enjoys some ancient central heating and double-glazing, thanks to a comfort-loving American bride who joined the family earlier this century. But what excites most people's curiosity is the rough, stone cell in which Edward II was reputedly held prisoner and horribly killed with a hot poker in 1327.

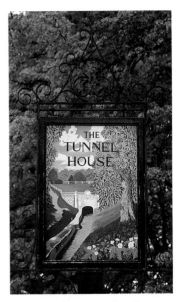

The Great Hall at Berkeley Castle   *The Tunnel House pub at Coates*

You have to take the guided tour which lasts about an hour, conducted in a cheerful, breezy style that some people enjoy and others find gratingly faux-naïf, as in, 'Well, Edward II, he certainly had a problem. And his problem was - too many favourites.' There is a self-service tea room, with outside seating, a gift shop, and access to lovely grounds (mostly terraced flower beds and lawns).

Connected to the castle but with its own ticket entry (adults 50p, children 20p), is the attractive **Butterfly Farm**, a hot and steamy tropical house, home to native and exotic species.

Berkeley Castle, signposted from M5, exit junction 13 or 14 and from A38. Tel: 0453 810332
Opening times: Apr, Tues-Sun 2-5pm; May-Sept, Tues-Sat 11am-5pm, Sun 2-5pm; Oct, Sun only 11am-5pm
Admission: adult £3.40; child £1.60

As you leave the castle, a footpath to the side of it takes you through the parish churchyard and into the chantry, now the **Jenner Museum**. Three rooms on the ground floor are dedicated to the life and work of Dr Edward Jenner who was born in the village in 1749 and worked from this house. The best known of his many achievements is the vaccine against smallpox - a disease which, in his time, accounted for about a third of all child deaths. The displays include papers and letters as well as some grisly photographs of smallpox sufferers. There is a re-creation of his elegant study and, in the garden, a thatched hut called the Temple of Vaccinia, where he vaccinated local people free of charge. Cuttings from a robust looking vine planted by Jenner are also for sale.

The Jenner Museum, The Chantry, Church Lane, Berkeley - access from M5, exit junction 13 or 14, or A38. Tel: 0453 810631
Opening times: Apr-Sept, Tues-Sat 12.30-5.30pm, Sun 1-5.30pm
Admission: adult £1.20; child 30p

COATES CANALSIDE WALK

For a good hour's walk, much of it along a canal, park your car at the Tunnel House Public House just outside Coates, in a lane off the Rodmarton Road. The landlord won't mind as long as you come in for a beer or cup of coffee. From the car park, a path leads down to the canal, now in the care of the Stroudwater, Thames and Severn Canal Trust. Both The Tunnel House pub at Coates and the Daneway, two miles away at Sapperton, were built for the benefit of the tunnellers at the end of the 18th century. Once you're down on the towpath, glance back at the wonderfully ornate entrance to the tunnel which runs to Sapperton.

When it was in active use, it was the longest in the country. It had no towpath and bargees had to propel their craft by lying on their backs and pushing against the tunnel roof with their feet for hours in the murky darkness. This was known as 'legging it' and often caused a severe back complaint called, 'lighterman's bottom'. Leggers often lost their balance and fell into the pitch black water.

Follow the path beside the canal. This short section of waterway has recently been cleared by volunteers. The rest is overgrown. Opinion is divided over whether it is more ecologically sound to clear the entire canal or leave well alone. As you deliberate this, you pass a strange round house, like a mini-lighthouse, on your right. Circular towers like this were built at regular intervals to house lengthsmen, who collected toll charges and maintained the canal. They often had families of 12 or more children who must have curled round each other to fit in.　　　　　→

When you come to a tiny stone bridge, leave the canal path by some steps to the right and cross the bridge. Pass through a farm gate and walk up the side of a field keeping the stone wall to your right. If you look back, you will see the line of trees marking the canal in the valley you have just left. At the top of the field, go over a stone stile and into the next field, keeping the stone wall on your left. At the top, you come to a tarred road. Turn left into the village of Coates and left again onto the Tarlton/Rodmarton Road. Walk down the hill until you get to the sign for the Tunnel House pub and follow the track back to the pub car park.

The Tunnel House is a good lunch-stop, not just for food, but for learning of other marvellous walking routes in the area - ask the landlord. In the summer, sausages and spare ribs are cooked on the outside barbecue. In winter, it's cosy sitting beside the carved wooden fireplace or looking out over a wooded landscape from the window seats. The same blackboard menu serves for lunch and dinner - last orders 2pm and 10pm. Real ales are Archers Best, Wadworths 6X and a varying 'guest' beer.

☆ SELSLEY HERB FARM

This used to be a herb and goat farm but the goats are slowly being phased out; the herbs, however, continue to grow from strength to strength. The farm is actually the large, well-stocked garden of a private house on the edge of Selsley Common. A long rose walk is festooned with old-fashioned roses underplanted with catmint; there's a sunken herb garden, some demonstration borders and a nursery. There are no less than 23 varieties of lavender and 16 varieties of rosemary for sale, along with variegated rue, curly woodsage, narrow leafed lungwort and mints.

The Wimperis family, whose garden this is, are great enthusiasts and happy to talk about their herbs and give advice on how to grow yours. Mr Wimperis started the business ten years ago and now supplies shops like Liberty and Heals. Mrs Wimperis gives talks and demonstrations to visiting groups on how to dry flowers, make pot pourris, grow and propagate herbs. Lectures are followed by a buffet supper and a glass of wine. A barn has been converted into a shop selling seeds, dried flowers, jams and chutneys. You'll find the same range of goods in the Selsley Herb Shop, owned by the family, in Nailsworth. Cream teas are served on Sunday afternoons. There are tremendous views of Rodborough Common from the garden.

Selsley Herb Farm, Water Lane, Selsley, off the B4066, south-west of Stroud. Tel: 0453 766682
Opening times: daily Apr-Sept, 10am-5pm; Sun 2-5pm
Admission: adult £1; child 50p

> For a browse around an old-fashioned antique and bric-a-brac shop, try **The Priory**, owned by J Vosper, in the lovely village of Minchinhampton. In five rooms stuffed full of china, glass, old photographs, brass, water colours, fans, washstands, Lloyd loom chairs, you really have the sensation you might find some little treasure.

SLIMBRIDGE WILDFOWL AND WETLANDS CENTRE

If you're wearing your leopard- or tiger-skin coat, stay away. Not surprisingly, given the conservation ethos of Slimbridge, founded in 1946 by the artist and naturalist, Sir Peter Scott, you won't be allowed in. The rest of us, though, could spend some happy hours here.

There are great numbers of migratory birds to this 880-acre park, as well as permanent residents such as pink flamingoes. What you see depends very much on the time of year. In spring, there are masses of newly hatched birds. In August, they begin to moult and are not at their most glamorous. It is in winter that the centre really comes into its own, with the arrival of migratory birds like the famous Bewick's Swans all the way from Siberia.

Whatever the season, there's much to look at and, particularly for children, plenty to do. Start by calling at the Information Desk which points out anything of current interest. There's bird food and a checklist of wildfowl for sale, binoculars and a cassette guide for hire. None of them is essential to enjoy the Centre, because everything is well signposted. The basic walk is a figure of eight around the ponds with points of interest explained along the way. You are welcome to use any of the several bird hides overlooking the Severn estuary.

If the weather is grim, head for the warmth of the Tropical House or stay inside the Visitor Centre to birdwatch through large picture windows. On wet days and at weekends, children are given paper and colouring pencils to draw and make brass rubbings. There is also a shop, self-service restaurant, good disabled access to all areas, including hides and the services of some extremely competent volunteer attendants.

The Wildfowl and Wetlands Centre, Slimbridge, signposted from M5, junctions 13 and 14, and from A38. Tel: 0453 890065
Opening times: daily 9.30am-5pm in summer, 9.30am-4pm in winter. Closed 24 & 25 Dec. No dogs
Admission: adult £4; child £2

Springtime at Slimbridge Wildfowl and Wetlands Trust

☆ STROUD

Stroud stands high on a hill at the meeting point of five valleys. It is distinguished among Cotswold towns as the only one touched by the industrial revolution - hence the gaunt mills along the valleys (now used for other light industrial projects), overgrown canals (some in the process of being rescued), derelict railway tracks (some now cycle paths). Stroud lacks the grandeur of Painswick and the static prettiness of the North Cotswold villages, having come of age in the utilitarian era of red brick and slate rather than stone. But it does have life, vigour, a hard-edged history, and it is surrounded by incomparably beautiful countryside. The austere buildings of the industrial age now seem an essential and lovely part of the landscape, as seen particularly in the neighbouring village of Chalford in the Golden Valley.

You can see the industrial history of the area exhibited in two distinct parts of the **Stroud Museum**. The main building on Lansdown is concerned with local geology and early history (a dusty jumble but well worth a potter). One room in this section has a collection that includes policeman's truncheons, traditional local pottery, and early lawnmowers of a sophistication that makes them hardly distinguishable from the modern variety. Look out for a couple of oil paintings which show fields laid out in a mosaic of red, blue, white and yellow cloth set to dry. The streams around here used to run with washed-out dye, particularly Stroudwater Scarlet, the dye that coloured the 'thin red line' of British army uniforms, which was Stroud's speciality. The nearby town of Uley provided 'Uley Blue' for naval uniforms. Nowadays, most of Stroud's mills have been turned to other uses, but Lodgemore Mill (not open to the public) still produces green baize for billiard tables, bright yellow cloth for tennis balls and good old Stroudwater Scarlet for Guards' uniforms.

Stroud from Rodborough

Tayloe's Mill, Chalford

The second part is the Industrial Museum. Turn right out of the main building, cross the street and go up some steps to reach it. Here you can see the old textile looms which brought wealth to some in Stroud and signalled a life of dreary hardship to many others. Rope- and barrel-making and walking-stick manufacture were Stroud specialities. The staff here are enthusiastic, but the premises are far too small to house a museum as important as Stroud's and there are moves afoot to transfer it, more appropriately, to a former mill.

Stroud has few fine buildings to admire, but you should see the 19th-century neo-classical Subscription Rooms in George Street, which also house the **Tourist Information Centre** (tel: 0453 765768) and, further up the hill, the late 16th-century Town Hall and the arcades of the former meat market, the Shambles.

The best café in Stroud is **Mother Nature** on Bedford Street just behind the Subscription Rooms. The daily specialities include a couple of main courses and lots of inventive and delicious salads. For a picnic, buy sandwiches and salads from here or from the sister shop, also called Mother Nature, in Russell Street.

☆ STROUD CIRCULAR DRIVE

This drive, of about 25 miles, touches on part of an officially designated scenic route. Leave Stroud on the A419 eastwards and follow the signs to King's Stanley, Leonard's Stanley and Frocester. See the vast National Trust tithe barn at Frocester, then take the Nympsfield road climbing steeply up the Cotswold escarpment (tremendous views back over your shoulder) to the B4066 which is the officially recognised scenic route. Turn right and very soon on your right, visible from the road, is a large neolithic burial chamber, **Uley Long Barrow**, otherwise known as Hetty Pegler's Tump. Walk along the edge of a field to get to it. You can peer into the entrance chamber but you would need a torch to explore any further.

Follow the road to **Uley**. The sign to 'The Brewery' leads to Uley Brewery (home of Pig's Ear, Old Spot, Uley Bitter and Pigor Mortis real ales). It is actually one of the outbuildings of a private house called Weavers Workshops, the others occupied by a wheelwright, a cabinet maker and Uley Carriage Hire, which rents horse-drawn caravans (made by the wheelwright) for holidays in this area (tel: 0453 860288).

> **Prema Arts Centre**, tucked in behind the main street in Uley, puts on excellent art and sculpture exhibitions and a lively programme of dance, theatre, and musical performances. You could join a video-making workshop or have a pottery or music lesson, paid for by the hour or half-hour. Open from 10am-6pm, Monday-Friday and for weekend and evening workshops and performances. Telephone the director, Liz Swift, on 0453 860703.

From Uley, follow the road to **Dursley**, the largest town in this area after Stroud. Look out for the painted statue of a particularly plump Queen Anne in a niche on the 18th-century Market House. You can divert here to Slimbridge or follow the road round westwards to Stinchcombe, North Nibley and Wotton-under-Edge. At **North Nibley** stands the monument - reminiscent of an industrial chimney - to William Tyndale who translated the New Testament into English. The energetic can climb to the monument and remains of the iron age settlement called Brackenbury Ditches.

Stroud's Town Crier

The Tyndale Monument at North Nibley

At Wotton-under-Edge, keep left on the B4058 and climb the escarpment once more. Join the A4135 briefly, then continue left-wards on B4058 to Nympsfield, then right on the B4066. Coaley Peak Picnic Site is on your left with spectacular views over the Severn estuary and the Forest of Dean. From here follow the road back to Stroud.

☆ **TETBURY**

Tetbury stands high on a busy crossroads just a few miles from the Wiltshire border, the tall spire of its parish church of St Mary visible for miles around. The possibility of seeing the Princesses Anne, Diana or Michael doing their shopping brings many a hopeful royal watcher here. But the real pleasure, as with many Cotswold towns, lies in strolling through the streets, recapturing a sense of the past and enjoying the present. There are enough inns and pubs to help you do all that.

Start with the **Market House/Town Hall**, bang in the centre,

The Market Hall at Dursley

from which all main streets diverge. Built in the mid-17th century as a Wednesday cloth market, its huge stone columns and arches support what looks like the suspended first floor of a substantial house, topped by a bell tower and weather vane of gambolling dolphins. It is still used as a market and general meeting place. The Women's Institute puts out its stalls on Friday.

Long Street, formerly full of smart antique shops in old 17th-century houses, is now only half-full of antique shops - those tough enough to have survived the recession - stocking, in general, high quality goods. Church Street leads to the **Church of St Mary**, unaccountably described by William Cobbett in his *Rural Rides* as 'a beautiful ancient church', though it was only 40 years old when he was writing in 1826. Its architect, Francis Hiorn has been described as 'one of the most accomplished designers of the elegant, decorative Gothic of the late 18th century, of which Tetbury church is an excellent example'. Tall windows, wooden pillars, panelled galleries and 18th-century candelabra are among its special features.

Church Street has two deservedly popular speciality shops: **Tetbury Traditional Meats**, at no. 31, sells handmade sausages, ranging from traditional pork to ham and apricot, and organic and free-range meat. The **House of Cheese**, at no. 13, sells over 100 varieties of cheese.

Chipping Street, just south from the Market House, leads to an open space called the Chipping, now a car park surrounded by 18th-century houses, but formerly the site of a cheese and bacon market - older than the central Market House. Chipping Steps, an ancient street so steep it had to be stepped, leads from here down to the River Avon, to two lovely looking houses, the Croft and Croft Cottage, at the bottom. Turn right and right again to climb back up to the Market Place via Gumstool Hill (gradient 1:4). This is where the Spring Bank Holiday Woolsack Races are run: young people race each other up the hill carrying 65lb sacks of wool on their backs.

(*i*) The Tetbury **Tourist Information Centre** (tel: 0666 503552) also houses a Police Bygones Museum - some cells and a collection of truncheons and handcuffs.

Badminton is the home of the racquet game. It is also home to the Duke of Beaufort, and the three-day international horse trials held in the spring. Walk down the main street of the little village of Great Badminton and see the extraordinary pinks, peaches and ochres of the houses here, more Italian than Cotswold. Almshouses, formerly built for the poor, bear shields and escutcheons of noble benefactors, which give them an aristocratic air. Badminton House is not open to the public but you can walk through the park from here to Little Badminton in 20 minutes.

⊙ ■ WESTONBIRT ARBORETUM

Like all well designed arboreta, Westonbirt appeals both to those who can recite the *Observer Book of Trees* and to those who merely 'quite like trees'. Just south of Tetbury, these 600 acres, now owned and developed by the Forestry Commission, were the creation and work of three generations of one family, the Holfords. Robert Holford planted the first tree in 1829 and now there are around 18,000 numbered species in the arboretum. This is probably one of the largest collections of trees and shrubs in the world thanks to the extent of the British Empire and the Victorian passion for collecting and travel.

The Visitor Centre has, quite deservedly, won awards for its design. The quality of the displays and interpretive material transforms a visit here. There's a current attractions board, suggested timed walks (bring sturdy shoes) and a full catalogue of all named trees in the arboretum. A cheery log fire welcomes winter visitors and a shop sells books, gifts and objects made of wood from the arboretum (wooden cut-out trees are very popular). Round the corner from the Visitor Centre, you'll find a snack bar and picnic site.

The park is so vast you may well wish to return at a different time of year (season tickets available). In the spring, people come for the flowering rhododendrons and azaleas but half the total number of annual visitors come in the autumn to see the maples and beeches turn colour - more New England than Old England Cotswold. At weekends throughout the year, special interest walks are laid on, often guided by the curator.

Westonbirt Arboretum, Tetbury, off the A433. Tel: 0666 88220
Opening times: Arboretum, daily 10am-8pm or sunset, whichever is earlier. The Visitor Centre and snack bar are open daily, 10am-5pm, from spring to autumn
Admission: adults £2; children £1

Silk Wood at Westonbirt Arboretum

WHERE TO STAY

Amberley

⌂ 🐕 ✉ ££

Hawthorns, *Lower Littleworth,*
Amberley, Stroud, Glos GL5 5AW
Tel: 0453 873535
Open Apr-Oct
Amberley is a tiny village on the
edge of Minchinhampton Common,
and Hawthorns is a large Queen
Anne house in the middle of it run
by Caroline Silver. There are two
double bedrooms with adjoining
bathrooms and a twin-bedded room
with its own separate bathroom.You
can sit out on the patio on summer
evenings and watch visiting badgers
and foxes. Caroline doesn't do
evening meals but the friendly Black
Horse pub, five minutes' walk away
on Minchinhampton Common,
serves good food at a reasonable
price.

Frocester

⌂ 🍴 🐕 ✉ £

Elmtree Farm, *Frocester, nr.*
Stonehouse, Glos GL10 3TG
Tel: 0453 823274
Open Apr-Oct
This farmhouse tucked beneath the
Cotswold escarpment has one double
room and two twin-bedded rooms
for guests. All have handbasins, tea-
and coffee-making facilities and are
decorated and furnished simply.
There is a large shared bathroom.
The facilities are simple - no telephone or TV in the bedrooms - and
the rates are good value. Jane Pain
does not offer evening meals but the
local pub, two minutes' walk away,
serves food. The Pains also grow 12
acres of flowers and grasses and offer
dried flowers for sale.

Owlpen

SC 🍴 🐕 ■ £££ - ££££

Owlpen Manor Cottages, *Owlpen*
Manor, nr Dursley, Glos GL11 5BZ
Tel: 0453 860261
Open all year
These cottages (three of them listed
buildings) cluster round a manor
house and church in the quiet, picturesque hamlet of Owlpen. They
range from The Gristmill (sleeps 8-9)
with much of its machinery intact, to
Peter's Nest Cottage, a perfect retreat
for two people. All are beautifully
decorated, furnished with modern
amenities including telephone and
TV, and each has a garden and parking space. Visitors can order gro-
ceries or home-made take-away food
from the manor kitchens. Minimum
stay of two nights.

Tetbury

⌂ ✕ 🍴10 ■ ££££

Calcot Manor, *nr Tetbury,*
Glos GL8 8YJ
Tel: 0666 890391
Open all year; R closed Sun eve
This large, Cotswold stone farmhouse near the junction of the A4135
and A46, south of Nailsworth, was
converted eight years ago into a luxury country house hotel and restaurant. In the 16 rooms (some in the
main house, others in restored outbuildings) the colour scheme is pastel
and floral, though each is decorated
differently. Bathrooms, almost as
large as the bedrooms, are particularly luxurious. There is a croquet lawn
and sheltered, heated swimming
pool in the garden.
Most people who stay at Calcot
choose to dine in the hotel's elegant
grey and peach dining room. Chef
Ramon Farthing serves classic
English and French food. Last orders:
lunch 2pm; dinner 9.30pm.

Tetbury
🏠 🧍 🐕 ✉ £££

Folly Farm Cottages, *Folly Farm, Tetbury, Glos GL8 8XA*
Tel: 0666 502475
Open all year
A minute's drive out of Tetbury on the Malmesbury road brings you to a complex of nine holiday cottages around a working dairy farm. With names like Cider Loft, Wheelwrights, Bull Pen, these are converted farmyard buildings of varying size, sleeping from two to ten. They are all well furnished and decorated with colour TV, double glazing and central heating. If your cottage has a wood burning stove as well, you are invited to help yourself, free of charge, from a log store. The Bentons, who run Folly Farm, maintain a cheerful but unobtrusive presence and you can be as sociable or reclusive as you like. A newspaper is delivered to your door every day and Tetbury is two minutes' walk away.

WHERE TO EAT

Nailsworth
🏠 ✕ ▭ ££

Egypt Mill, *Nailsworth*
Tel: 0453 833449
Open all year
The food here is good, though not adventurous (steaks and pizzas a speciality) and the prices are not high. But it's the surroundings that make eating here such a pleasure: Egypt Mill was a 14th-century corn mill, rebuilt and extended over the centuries into a cloth mill, then converted in 1985 into a restaurant, using only old timbers. Its mill pond and water wheels are intact. The outbuildings are now hotel rooms. There is no shortage of space, with several bars, a huge lounge on the first floor and two restaurant areas. Last orders: lunch 1.45pm; dinner 9.45pm.

Nailsworth
✕ ▭ ££

Tubby's Café, *28 George Street, Nailsworth, Stroud*
Tel: 0453 834802
Open all year: Mon-Sat 8.30am-5pm;
Sat eve from 8pm
Tubby's premises are frankly too small for the number of customers but the food is delicious and such good value that nobody minds sitting in a comradely huddle. Try the butter bean and tomato soup. It's counter service during the day. Lunches have a strong vegetarian bias but always include one meat dish: last orders 2pm. Dinner is a single sitting on Saturday evening with waitress service.

Nailsworth
✕ ▭ ££

William's Bistro, *3 Fountain Street, Nailsworth*
Tel: 0453 832240
Open all year, Tues-Sat dinner only
William's Bistro is behind William's Kitchen which is an excellent deli cum fish shop. Try the mixed seafood platter for £17.50. Meat eaters are also well catered for. The wine list is sensibly brief, with the house wine selling at £7 a bottle. Last orders 9.30pm.

BATH AND THE
SOUTHERN WOLDS

The southern tip of the Cotswolds ends with the city of Bath, a fitting climax to a week's tour, especially at Festival time in June. A quick run through the principal sights of Bath - the Roman Baths and Pump Room, Royal Crescent, the Museum of Costume in the Assembly Rooms - would occupy the whole day, hardly giving you a moment to soak up the city's Georgian splendours. Then there are the shops, the restaurants, a stroll by the canal, an evening at the Theatre Royal and a boat trip to squeeze in.

If you've fallen in love with the golden look of Bath, a visit to Corsham to see the source of the local stone will be of special interest. Both Corsham Court and Dyrham Park are fine manor houses within half an hour's drive of the city. And although you are far south here you haven't left the picture postcard Cotswolds behind. The film of *Dr Doolittle* was shot in the village of Castle Combe, transformed into a seaport despite the total absence of sea - and all because it was so pretty. In addition, because Castle Combe has never been developed, it looks exactly as it must have done in the middle of the 15th century, with a tiny market place, two inns and a main street lined with houses. Whatever else you do and whatever the weather, don't miss a visit to the American Museum at Claverton, two miles east of Bath.

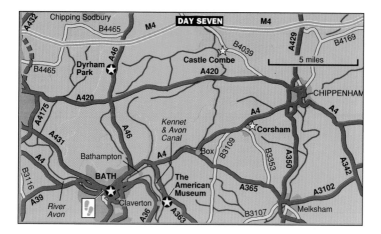

THE AMERICAN MUSEUM

No ordinary museum, this is a vivid celebration of American art and craft from the arrival of the first Puritans from England to the mid-19th century. Two Americans, Dallas Pratt and the late John Judkyn, chose a neo-classical manor at Claverton to house displays which they hoped would illustrate Anglo-American continuity and promote mutual understanding.

You begin by walking through a series of rooms, furnished to reflect different periods and styles of living. Everything is authentic - from the dimensions of the rooms to furniture and furnishings, floorboards and panelling, most of it brought from the United States. Look out for the flamboyant New Orleans bedroom from the time of the Civil War, the walls, furniture and furnishings entirely decorated in stencils. The collection of textiles, particularly the patchwork quilts, are minor artworks.

The lives of the early settlers, the cowboys, the men who worked on whaling ships, American Indians and Hispanics are all celebrated here. There are displays of pistols worn by cowboys, an ivory measuring instrument that belonged to a Chinese gold prospector, a Wells Fargo stage coach strong box. Indian silver and beadwork is particularly fine.

Try an American cookie or a slice of George Washington's

17th-century room in The American Museum in Britain

favourite cake, made to his cook's recipe, also on sale. And don't neglect the displays in the grounds - the wagon, tepee, herb shop, the replica of Washington's garden at Mount Vernon, and particularly the Folk Art Gallery. The guides are all local volunteers and all, to a woman, extremely good.

The American Museum in Britain, Claverton Manor, Bath, signposted from A36. Tel: 0225 460503
Opening times: daily except Mon, beg Apr-end Oct, 2-5pm; Sun and Bank Hol Mons 11am-5pm; gardens daily except Mon 1-6pm
Admission: house, grounds and galleries: adult £4.50; child £2.50; grounds and Folk Art Museum: adult £1.50; child £1

✪ BATH

A Georgian city built inside a bowl of hills and skirted by the river Avon, Bath has been a tourist attraction for centuries. The Romans built a temple, baths and a city round its hot springs, calling it Aquae Sulis, after a Celtic deity. In the 18th century, smart folk came to 'take the waters' which continued to gush out of the ground at a rate of half a million gallons a day and, at a constant steaming 116°F. John Wood the elder, early architect of Bath, wrote about the additional inducements of 'Cheap Provisions, Healthy Walks, Polite Society and Many Families of Distinction'.

The Georgian heyday of Bath lasted only about 60 years from the 1720s. But it was this period which shaped the city streets and buildings in an architectural style that everybody comes to see. Then there are the associations with Jane Austen, Beau Nash, Samuel Pepys. Names like the Bath Oliver biscuit and the Bath bun make us feel we know the city even before we arrive.

The best way to see Bath is to take a free guided walk, entertaining as well as informative and leaving from outside the Pump Room at 10.30am and 2pm every day. The open-top bus tours with microphone commentary may be a useful way of getting to The American Museum if you have no transport of your own, but otherwise they are unnecessarily intrusive and best avoided. Don't bother with the Ghost Walk, either: Bath is too light and cheerful a place to harbour decent ghosts.

(i) After the **Tourist Information Centre** (tel: 0225 462831) in The Colonnades, Bath Street, the **Roman Baths Museum and Pump Room** nearby are everybody's first stop. Begin with a walk through the museum which is particularly good on the excavation of its Roman remains and makes sense of the rest of your visit. The Romans used the hot springs as a bath (warm, hot, cold, sauna and massage) and also as a place of entertainment and worship. A temple to the goddess Sulis Minerva was excavated in the first half of the 18th century, and the collection of Roman votive offerings found there is the best in England. Curses written on sheets of pewter and thrown into the Sacred Spring for divine consideration include a plea that the thief of a pair of gloves 'should lose his mind and his eyes' or that a horse thief should become impotent and die.

Leave the museum at the entrance to the Great Baths, the original swimming pool, opened to the sky by the Victorians - hence the green colour from growth of algae - and decorated atop with statues of Roman emperors. Guided tours of the whole bath complex begin here every 20 minutes.

The tour ends in the Pump Room, a medicinal and social centre built in 1791. Listen to the music of a trio while you sip some curative spring water. If it smells like bad eggs, remember it's rain water that has been in the ground for 10,000 years. Surveying the scene is the statue of Richard 'Beau' Nash who arrived in Bath in 1704 and was appointed Master of Ceremonies to organise its hitherto rather disreputable social life. The spa water had always been used as a cure for venereal diseases and John Wood, Bath's greatest architect, complained in pre-Nash days of 'people of both sexes bathing by day and night naked; and dogs, cats, pigs and even human creatures hurl'd over the rails into the water'. Nash insisted on formal standards of dress and behaviour, forbade loud music late at night, outlawed over-charging among sedan chair attendants and generally raised the tone of the place.

Roman Baths Museum, The Pump Room, Bath. Tel: 0225 461111 ext. 2785
Opening times: daily Mar-Oct 9am-6pm, Jul & Aug 9am-7pm, Nov-Feb 9am (Sun 10am)-5pm
Admission: adult £3.80; child £1.80; combined ticket for Roman Baths and Costume Museum: adult £4.60; child £2.30

The Roman Baths in Bath

To your right as you emerge from the Pump Room stands **Bath Abbey**, built mostly in 15th-century Perpendicular style and famous for its clerestory windows and fan vaulting. Look out for the memorial tablets to Beau Nash, Isaac Pitman, the inventor of shorthand, and Dr Oliver, creator of the Bath Oliver biscuit.

Abbey Green, south of the Abbey, is a delightful, shady, pre-Georgian square (rare in this city), once a bowling green for the Abbey's monks. The Crystal Palace pub in a corner, so called after the Crystal Palace in London, was formerly a private house where Lord Nelson stayed to recuperate from wounds sustained in the Battle of the Nile.

Sally Lunn's House at North Parade Passage (formerly Old Lilliput Alley, a much more apt name) is reckoned to be the oldest residential building in Bath, dating from 1482. The original Sally Lunn was a French Huguenot, Solange Luyon, who came to Bath in 1680 and became a baker. Now, the house is a well promoted tourist spot satisfactorily viewed from outside, unless you're dying for a Sally Lunn (Bath) bun. There is a coffee room on the ground floor, a small restaurant on the first, and a small basement shop/museum.

To see the best of Georgian Bath begin at the north side of **Queen's Square**: no. 24 was the home of Bath's foremost architect, John Wood the elder; Jane Austen often visited her brother at no. 13. Continuing northwards, no. 41 Gay Street was the home of John Wood the younger, now insurance offices. Peep into the tiny front room decorated with blue and white tiles. This was the powder room where men powdered their wigs before they joined the party. At the top of Gay Street, you come to **The Circus**, three curved terraces forming a perfect circle. The sequence of columns: Doric on the ground floor, then Ionic, then Corinthian at the top, is a standard 18th-century pattern. Left at the Circus brings you to Brock Street and thence to the immense curve of the **Royal Crescent**, 30 terraced houses, and one of the most famous pieces of domestic architecture in the world.

Many luminaries have lived in the Royal Crescent - William Pitt the elder at no. 7, David Livingstone at no. 13, and Thomas Gainsborough at no. 17 to name but three. The house at **No. 1 Royal Crescent** is open to the public, painstakingly restored, furnished and decorated by the Bath Preservation Trust in the manner of the 18th century. The amount of bare floorboards and the brightness of the colours are at first surprising. Visitors may have to content themselves with peering round doors to see inside the rooms because so much is roped off, and you may find the atmosphere the teeniest bit reverential. Visit the kitchen downstairs to see how 18th-century households turned their roasting spits, using an unholy combination of a dog inside a wheel and a piece of hot coal to keep everything moving.

No. 1 Royal Crescent, Bath. Tel: 0225 428126
Opening times: Mar-Oct, Tues-Sun and Bank Hol Mons 11am-5pm; Nov-Dec 11am-4pm
Admission: adult £3; child £2

At the north-western exit of The Circus, at Bennett Street, you will find the **Assembly Rooms**, designed by John Wood the younger. It now houses the excellent **Museum of Costume** and the Fashion Research Centre. The displays are comprehensive, covering 400 years of fashion and ending in the current 'dress of the year'. Although there are clothes from the 16th and 17th century (including a rare woman's dress from the 1660s), the majority of items date from the 18th century onwards. Even so, the museum has the space to display only a tenth of its collection at any one time. It's worth taking the guided tour (included in price of ticket, lasts half an hour) to get your money's worth. The Museum also runs a Fashion Research Centre, open to the public, at 4 Circus.

Museum of Costume and Assembly Rooms, Bennett Street, Bath. Tel: 0225 461111
Opening times: daily Mar-Oct 9.30am-6pm (Sun 10am-6pm); Nov-Feb 10am-5pm (Sun 11am-5pm)
Admission: adult £2.40; child £1.55; combined ticket for Costume and Roman Baths Museums: adult £4.60; child £2.30

A perfect summer lunch spot - complete with flowers and fountains - is **The Moon and Sixpence** in Broad Street which offers an excellent self-service buffet from noon-2.30pm. A perfect winter lunch spot is the **Paragon Bistro and Bar** in the Paragon, a cosy, intimate place with roaring fires. Its specialities are Breton *crêpes* and home-made soup, served from noon-2.30pm.

However short your visit to Bath, don't miss the **Industrial Heritage Centre** in Julian Road, a wonderfully quirky museum of the several businesses run by a family named Bowler from 1872. They were engineers, involved in the excavation of the Roman Baths and the laying of the first gas pipes in the city, while also running a brass foundry and soda water factory from the same premises. Their business methods were a curator's joy. Every invoice and letter was kept, including notes like this from a hairdresser in 1884: 'My Hair-Brushing Machine has gone wrong and I am unable to use it. Please send a man up today and oblige.' Every tool and piece of machinery was preserved in its original state. Nothing was thrown away and nothing updated. The firm ceased trading in 1969, ground to a halt, one suspects, by the accumulated detritus of nearly a hundred years.

Don't miss, either, the delightful **Museum of English Naïve Art** in the Paragon. All the objects or paintings, by travelling artists and workmen, 1750-1900, are simple, charming and sometimes hilarious. It may sound unlikely to non-philatelists, but you could also spend a couple of happy hours in **Bath Postal Museum** in Broad Street. Did you know that the first ever stamped letter was probably sent from this very address? Or that, from 1868, all general post offices in England had cats on the payroll? And the mail always seemed to get through: letters recovered from ships sunk at sea or part-burnt in fires were nevertheless sent - and received. If the refreshment room is unmanned, make your own cup of tea - the milk's in the fridge. Anyone seriously interested in photography should visit the **The National Centre for Photography** in Milsom Street and theatre lovers must call in at the **Theatre Royal**, Sawclose.

The best way to get away from the crowds in Bath is to walk along the canal towpath from Pulteney Bridge or take a boat trip from Pulteney Weir to Bathampton. You can also spend an afternoon punting from the elegant Victorian Boating Station at Forester Road, a 20-minute walk from the town centre or a free boat trip from Pulteney Weir. Tuition is free.

Anything you can buy in London, you can buy more comfortably in Bath. Here's a brief guide to some of the best shops. Try Guinea Lane for antiques on Wednesday morning; get here early before the dealers. Walcot Reclamations on Walcot Street sells brass fingerplates, fire irons, cast iron baths, anything for the older house. For the smaller house, The China Doll, also in Walcot, has the most comprehensive collection of doll's house furniture imaginable, including long-stemmed wine glasses. Buy your French and Italian clothes from Catch 22 on Broad Street, cheeses from Langmans in John Street or The Fine Cheese Company in Walcot Street (also pâtés and mouthwatering olive, walnut, onion and hazelnut breads), second-hand designer clothes from Gearchange in Rivers Street and delicious hamburgers from Schwartz Bros on Walcot. If it's a transformation you're after, Make Over in Upper Borough Walls will make you up into something your own mother won't recognise and then photograph you.

BATH CANALSIDE WALK

Leave the centre of town by Pulteney Bridge, designed by Robert Adam in 1774, and continue straight down Great Pulteney Street. This area was designed by Thomas Baldwin between 1788 and 1790 in the hope of making the east side of the river as grand as the Upper Town. Too late - Bath was already losing its fashionable status.

At the end of Great Pulteney Street are Sydney Gardens and the **Holbourne Museum and Crafts Centre**, another great Bath museum. If you decide to stop off here, you will find a collection of 18th-century porcelain and silver (look out for the Meissen chamberpot carried by women in their muffs for emergencies), 18th-century furniture and paintings, including some Gainsborough, Reynolds and Raeburn portraits. The museum, small and varied enough to avoid visual indigestion, is closed from mid-December to mid-February. The Tea House, a charming little pavilion in the garden behind the museum, serves refreshments and light lunches. Open 11am-5pm, Sunday 2.30-5pm.

Walk northwards through Sydney Gardens, over the railway bridge to the towpath of the Kennet and Avon canal. Fields rise high on the right with views of distant houses on the ridge. And to the left, the land falls to the Great Western Railway line and, beyond, to the river Avon. Watch out for cyclists who also use the towpath. As you approach the village of Bathampton, The George pub on your left is a good and often busy refreshment stop. Last orders: lunch 2pm; dinner 9.30pm. Gnomes have taken over the garden of the house opposite. Return by the same route.

Pulteney Bridge, Bath

☆ CASTLE COMBE

Castle Combe follows the tradition of picturesque Cotswold villages in every particular, even to the extent of being endlessly filmed and photographed. Approached from the B4039 through a winding wooded valley, the village is a sweet cluster of ancient stone buildings around a central roofed market cross, with a river flowing through at the bottom. There are a couple of pubs (The White Hart is recommended), a church, a manor house, now a luxurious country hotel, and extremely restricted parking.

Again, in a typically Cotswold, small but sophisticated village, you'll find shops ranging from an old-fashioned post office to a gift shop which sells, among other things, American hand-crafted wood, to Michel Le Coz's four-poster bed workshop. So, if you've always wanted a four-poster and have around £1,500-£2,000 to spare, you've come to the right place. The beds are all hand-turned and hand-carved. Hangings, quilts and hand-crocheted bedspreads are also made here.

A rare glimpse of Castle Combe deserted

Corsham Court

☆ CORSHAM

A prosperous looking village on the A4 some ten miles north-east of Bath, Corsham is worth visiting for its wide High Street and fine 17th- and 18th-century houses in pale grey stone. The most substantial building of them all, **Corsham Court**, stands at one end of the village. This Elizabethan house was bought by Paul Methuen in the middle of the 18th century to house his collection of paintings, mostly of the Italian and Flemish schools. As the collection grew to include Dutch and English works, so the house was altered and extended.

The State Rooms, including the Music Room, Dining Room and Picture Gallery, are all on the ground floor on either side of the entrance hall. There is some grand furniture on display as well as paintings like *The Annunciation*, from the studio of Fra Filippo, and *The Betrayal* by Van Dyck. A charming study of the Methuen children by Joshua Reynolds hangs in the dining room.

Capability Brown and Humphrey Repton designed the gardens and the amusing stone Gothic Bath House. Staff at the manor recall tales of the present Lord Methuen's grandfather, 'The Field Marshall' (the family was ennobled in 1838), using it regularly for an early morning cold plunge, a servant stationed outside with a red flag to ensure privacy.

Corsham Court, Corsham, off the A4. Tel: 0249 712214
Opening times: daily, except Mon and Fri, Jan 1-Nov 30 2-4.30 pm; Good Fri-Sept 30,
daily except Mon 2-6pm
Admission: adult £3; child £1.50

The **Underground Quarry Centre** at Corsham is the only shaft stone mine in Britain - albeit not a working one. The enterprise, newly launched by ex-engineer David Pollard and his wife, Nina Roberts, gives us a chance to see where the magical Cotswold stone came from. David is an enthusiastic guide, tempering technical information with breezy anecdote.

Armed with helmet and lamp, you descend 159 steps (remember there's no lift for coming up again) and walk through tunnels and galleries once quarried for stone. Dress warmly: the temperature is a constant 51°F throughout the year. Try your hand at sawing the stone - it's surprisingly easy. Taste it - according to David Pollard, the crushed limestone was used to supplement flour in breadmaking during the war. You can see the calculations quarrymen made of their day's work on the walls - they were paid according to how much they'd cut out - as well as graffiti (inoffensive) left by workers when it was used during the war as a naval ammunition dump. Tours last one hour and the first begins at 10.15am, 11.45am on Saturday. Last tour 3.30pm.

The Underground Quarry Centre, Park Lane, Corsham - access from A4. Tel: 0249
716288
Opening times: May-Aug, daily except Fri; Apr, Sept & Oct, Sun & Easter Mon only
Admission: adult £3.20; child £1.80

✪ DYRHAM PARK

Dyrham Park is a curiosity - an English mansion in 17th-century Dutch style - eight miles north of Bath. The name 'Dyrham' means 'deer enclosure' and deer (as well as a few cows) roam the grounds as you approach the house. Originally, the house belonged to the Winter family whose daughter, Mary, married William Blathwayt, a career diplomat, in 1686. She died soon afterwards but her husband went on to attain high office under the Dutch King William III. In the course of his work he travelled

Sawing limestone at Corsham Underground Quarry Centre

frequently between England and Holland and, in whatever spare time he had, he rebuilt Dyrham, much of it in the Dutch manner. The beginnings were modest but as his own fortunes grew, he employed the services of the court architect, William Talman.

Although Blathwayt's descendants continued to live at Dyrham until the 1950s, when the National Trust took over the property, Blathwayt's own legacy of decoration and furnishings has remained. The walnut and cedar staircases recall his position as Commissioner of Trade and Plantations. The stamped Dutch leather hangings in the East Hall were bought by Blathwayt on a visit to the Hague in 1700. His bitter complaints against his workmen have a timeless ring: 'Hunter [the joiner] intends never to have finished but to loiter in the country at my expense'.

There is a great deal of blue and white Delft ware and tulip vases, a clever perspective painting - *View down a Corridor* - by van Hoogstraten, fine painted ceilings, a Murillo of *Peasant Woman and Boy*, Flemish tapestries, rococo mirrors and some grand furniture. From a much later period, there is an interesting display of intricately embroidered aprons, banned by Beau Nash as evening wear from Bath society.

The terraced gardens bear little resemblance to their original Dutch design. A single statue of Neptune standing on a rise overlooking the house is all that remains of the pools, fountains and cascades of the original water garden.

The explanatory leaflet that comes with your ticket is adequate to enjoy the house but there is a guide book for sale, taped cassettes to hire and special guide books for children. The Orangery serves light lunches (noon-2.15pm) and teas (2.15-5pm). No dogs are allowed in the deer park.

Dyrham Park, Dyrham, signposted from A46. Tel: 0275 822501
Opening times: park all year, noon-5.30pm; house, Mar 30-Nov 3, daily except Thurs & Fri, noon-5.30pm. Last admission, 30 mins before closing
Admission: adult £4.40; child £2.20

WHERE TO STAY

Bath
🏠 ✕ 👤 🐎 🛏 **££££**

Bath Spa Hotel, *Sydney Road, Bath, Avon BA2 6JF*
Tel: 0225 444006
Open all year
Bath's new luxury class hotel is a restored 19th-century neo-classical mansion set on a wooded hill ten minutes' walk from the city centre. The management aims to provide 'refined hospitality' with thick carpets, bedrooms mainly decorated in plain or Regency striped walls with colourful floral furnishing fabrics and huge bathrooms in marble and mahogany. The public rooms, including the Vellore dining room (open to non-residents) are all grand. There's a swimming pool, sauna, solarium and gym inside, and a ten-

nis and croquet lawn outside. Children under 10 have special meal times and menus.

Bath
🏠 👤 ✉ **££**

Brock's Guest House, *32 Brock Street, Bath, Avon BA1 2LN*
Tel: 0225 338374
Often closed in January for about 2 wks for re-decoration
Arguably the friendliest b&b accommodation in town, this 18th-century house is just one minute's walk from Royal Crescent and run by Marion Dodd with the assistance of her mother. The accommodation is varied - two large, comfortable, double rooms (can be family rooms) with bath and shower, two double and

two twin-bedded rooms with shower, and two single rooms with hand basins but no private bathroom. They are all attractively decorated and equipped with TV, tea- and coffee-making facilities and hair-dryers. Guests are invited to use the spacious sitting room downstairs.

Bathampton
🏠 🧍 🐾 ▭ ££

Appletree Cottage, *Bathampton, nr Bath. Rented through Town and Country Cottages, 22 Charmouth Road, Newbridge, Bath, Avon BA1 3LJ. Tel: 0225 481764*
Available all year
This terraced cottage is in the centre of Bathampton village, ten minutes' drive from Bath. Walk through the front door directly into the sitting room. The dining room beyond leads into a well equipped kitchen with a breakfast bar. Upstairs there is a double bedroom, twin-bedded room and bathroom, all simply but well decorated. The long, narrow back garden, apart from the large apple tree which gives the cottage its name, is mostly lawn and ends at the edge of the Kennet and Avon canal. A quiet and beautiful spot but dangerous for unsupervised toddlers.

Box
🏠 🧍 🐾 ✉ £

Saltbox Farm, *Drewitts Mill, Box, Corsham, Wilts SN14 9PT*
Tel: 0225 742608
Open all year

Those who value peace and quiet will enjoy this 18th-century farmhouse, tucked away in the rural fastnesses of the Box Valley. Mrs Gregory offers one double and one twin-bedded room with handbasins, tea- and coffee-making facilities, and a guest bathroom. Views from both rooms are delightfully pastoral. Mrs Gregory plans to offer evening meals but, at present, guests have to drive to a nearby pub in Box or Colerne. There are reductions for stays of more than one night.

Castle Combe
🏠 ✕ 🧍 🐾 ▭ ££££

The Manor House, *Castle Combe, Chippenham, Wilts SN14 7HR*
Tel: 0249 782206
Open all year
This mostly 16th-century manor house, set in 26 acres of gardens and wooded grounds, is for those who like luxurious living in a country setting. The public rooms are grand, with huge stone fireplaces and panelled walls. De luxe bedrooms have a liberal scatter of antique furniture, four-poster beds, whirlpool baths. The extra accommodation in nearby stone cottages is only slightly less grand. Mid-week visitors may find the house bustling with business conferences but weekends are generally for the sybaritic. There is a hard tennis court, croquet lawn, heated outdoor pool and opportunities for trout fishing in Bybrook river.

WHERE TO EAT

Bath
✕ ▭ **£££**

Beaujolais, *5A Chapel Row, Queen Square, Bath*
Tel: 0225 423417
Closed Sun & Bank Hol Mon

The enduring popularity of the Beaujolais owes much to the lively, idiosyncratic manner of its proprietor, Jean-Pierre Auge - the sort of person to draw up a chair and join you for dinner if it suits him. The atmosphere is informal, the food is good French cooking, nothing fancy. An evening is judged a success at Beaujolais if everyone staggers out at the end amid continuing conversation and laughter. Last orders: lunch 2pm; dinner 10.30pm (Sat 11pm).

Bath
✕ ▭ **£££**

The Circus Restaurant, *34 Brock Street, Bath*
Tel: 0225 330208
Closed Sun dinner

Just down Brock Street from the Royal Circus, the Circus Restaurant is on two floors, elegant with small tables, bentwood chairs and potted palms. The menu is a varied one - crispy roast duck in sweet and sour sauce, or roast rack of lamb with ratatouille and rosemary sauce. Lunch can be light and quick while dinner is an evening-long affair. Last orders: lunch 2.30pm; dinner till late.

Bath
✕ ▭ **£££**

Claret's Restaurant and Wine Bar, *7a Kingsmead Square, Bath*
Tel: 0225 466688
Closed Sun

The basement of a Georgian house in a pretty square, Claret's is all in chaste white and black with just a dash of claret. If you can get past names on the menu like Munchie Mushrooms (sautéed mushrooms) and Supremely Satisfying (breast of chicken), the food itself is very good. Those intending to dash off after the main course to take in a play or a concert and return to finish their meal should ask to join Claret's Curtain Call Club for the evening. Last orders: lunch 2pm; dinner 10.30pm (Fri & Sat 11pm).

Bath
✕ ▭ **£££**

Woods, *9-13 Alfred Street, Bath*
Tel: 0225 314812
Closed Sun and Dec 24-29

This restaurant-brasserie, close to the Assembly Rooms, is a cheerful meeting place. The bar and brasserie section leads to the main restaurant decorated in horse racing theme, reflecting the passion of owner David Price. There is a choice of set-price menus, including a two-course menu for early diners (between 6.30-7.30pm), *à la carte* and blackboard specials. Last orders: restaurant - lunch 2.30pm; dinner 10.30pm; brasserie open 11am-11pm.